Norfolk Fragments

Norfolk Fragments

Bruce Robinson

Elmstead Publications,

Wicklewood, Norfolk, NR18 9QL

Published 1994

Elmstead Publications, Elmstead, Milestone Lane, Wicklewood, Norfolk, NR18 9QL

First published 1994

ISBN 0 9523379 0 8

Text and book design by the author using a DTP system with Aldus PageMaker 5. Main text font: Arial.

Printed by Geo. Reeve Ltd, Wymondham, Norfolk.

Orders to the publisher. Cheques: Elmstead Publications. Please add £1 for postage and packing.

Photographs: Bruce Robinson. Cover illustration: Wall plaques at Burston Strike School.

Contents

Foreword

Even when we were covering the Division Two Canaries together I could tell Bruce Robinson was a First Division magpie . . . He picked up what most would dismiss as unconsidered trifles and took them back to line his nest. He knew they would come in handy one day.

This tantalising volume represents just part of that collection of the curious, the eccentric and the interesting. I reckon it all helped to keep him smiling when the football fare was dull at Carrow Road or other emporiums of sporting entertainment. Or when his beloved Charlton were struggling to rediscover the form that brought FA Cup glory just after the last war.

To say Bruce exuded a scholarly air on the local reporting circuit is not to accuse him of being aloof or superior; it was just that he showed so much interest in so many subjects, questioning where others would meekly accept and storing away what most would blithely disregard.

The value of such a policy was underlined when he switched to different branches of journalism, perhaps most notably with the Clement Court column in the Eastern Daily Press, and when he decided to sift through piles of raw material to turn them into books.

From Hitler's Oak at How Hill to the "hospital" on Dogger Bank where fishermen believe the sick fish go, this catalogue of the unusual will constantly delight and amuse - and occasionally amaze.

Did you know Manor Farm at Bale boasted a four-hole outside toilet? Or that Flowerpot Man was a member of a local lifeboat crew, and Marmeduke Bootflower a resident of King's Lynn?

Plenty of other colourful characters await your inspection. I can add a personal salute towards Jack Murton, who delivered newspapers for 72 years, starting on the day world war one broke out. Jack's round included my home village of Beeston in mid-Norfolk . . . and I can still see his bike and smile and hear his whistle and cheery voice.

Norfolk Fragments pieced together into a memorable mosaic. The promise of more from Bruce the magpie is an alluring one.

Keith Skipper

(BBC Radio Norfolk)
Cromer, 1994

Introduction

This book is intended as a sort of guide to Norfolk and certain border territories. But it is not a guidebook. Let me make that plain from the start. Rather, it is a collection of the eccentric, the curious and the interesting; in other words, a kind of catalogue of uniqueness.

Nor does the book make any claim to completeness. This would have required a thoroughly painstaking approach, whereas I have been rather more interested in entries which simply intrigued or amused. For example, there is comparatively little from our towns and city, and only a light dusting of that which is historical. I bequeath these tasks to someone else.

In the beginning it emanated from a personal trawl through fragments of information remembered and collected during more than 30 years in Norfolk journalism; a hobby inspired partly by the area's continuing reluctance to depart completely from its traditional "du different" stance, despite innumerable pressures, and partly by my own particular brand of whimsy.

More than anything else, the book represents a personal selection of some of the bits and pieces and items which have fascinated me over the years and which I wanted to write up because of the realisation that nothing is permanent and that one day I might lose all the boxes of cuttings, files, references, scribbled notes and recollections within which the essence and the ideas were preserved.

I hope you like them.

Finally, my grateful thanks for the Foreword to former journalistic colleague and long-time friend Keith Skipper, whose Radio Norfolk programmes overflow with his particular brand of whimsy (and whose postcode, deliciously, ends in DJ); to Bob Bagshaw, of Wymondham, for his advice; to Brian Seager of George Reeve Ltd, Wymondham, for smoothing out the printing bumps and thus convincing me that desk top publishing was a real possibility; and to GST Training (Peterborough), David Robinson and John Bowman for patiently teaching me which buttons to press, and in what order.

Bruce Robinson

Wicklewood, 1994

In the 1930s one national newspaper described Gimingham as "the strangest village in England." (See Bits and Pieces). It still has an engine as its village sign.

This unusual bridge in the grounds of the Priory at Walsingham may have been built for the convenience of packhorses.

1: Setting the Scene

The design of the East Anglian flag unites the shield of St Edmund and three golden crowns - representing the under-kings of the South, North and Cambridge folk - with the cross of St George. It is entirely unofficial and was evidently dreamed up by the East Anglian Society when its committee, which included Prince Frederick Duleep Singh, approved a design by George Langham. The flag is thought to have flown for the first time from the tower of Sandringham church in 1919.

East Anglia was already largely converted to Christianity in the 7th century when the bishopric was divided into a southern sector based on Dunwich or Felixstowe, and a northern sector, possibly administered from North Elmham. The creation of North folk and South folk (Norfolk and Suffolk) seems to date from about this time. The earliest known written reference to "Norfolke" appears in a will dated in the 1040s.

The name of Norwich has been spotted on a coin of King Athelstan minted around AD930. Against that, in 1988 a member of the Norfolk Astrological Society said she had plotted the city's birth chart. Evidently a Taurean city, it was born on May 4, 1194, at 33 hours 54 minutes and 48 seconds exactly.

Norfolk's 1,307,333 acres - it is the fourth largest English county, behind Yorkshire, Lincolnshire and Devon - are home to some 750,700 people, and many think this is enough. In the past, letters to the Eastern Daily Press have discussed declarations of independence, a tax on "furriners," the erection of border customs posts, and the conversion of the A17 Nene river bridge at Sutton Bridge - just over the border in nearby Lincolnshire - from swing to drawbridge. A few years ago Beetley, near Dereham, even formed a village association to help build bridges between natives and incomers.

Critics say Norfolk is "a graveyard of ambition" - usually omitting to add it is because it is such a nice place to live. Locals tend to enjoy this sort of snobbery. Some still insist on saying they are going "down" to London, and at Liverpool Street railway station or Victoria coach depot that they are coming "up" to Norwich.

A Norfolk artist once urged the indigenous population to adopt a higher "visibility" in response to social change. He designed a Certificate of Norfolkmanship which referred to birth in "God's realm, hereinafter referred to as Norfolk," as "an honour most highly coveted and withheld from most by the Lord in his wisdom." Some rules can be very tight. For example, in order to qualify as a Shannock, traditionalists say you need to have been born in Sheringham of Sheringham-born parents.

Everyone likes to think they are at the centre of things. East Dereham claims to be the "Heart of Norfolk" even though the geographical centre of the county, if you cut out its boundaries in cardboard and spin it on a pin, is probably closer to Watton.

In fact we are all closer to the county than we think. An optician acquaintance once pointed out that the fundus (inside rear) of the eye resembled a "map" of Norfolk. Even the city and ring road systems are evidently recognisible among the veins and arteries when viewed through an ophthalmoscope. On request, he would conduct an examination by "travelling" the Fakenham road to Wells, the Yarmouth road, or even down the A11. I forgot to ask about the southern bypass.

Between 1971 and 1984 the county's population increased by 11 per cent with an annual inward movement of about 5000 people. Norfolk County Council, on the other hand, worked out that half the new arrivals were over the age of 50. Pensioners currently make up about 22 per cent of the population, with women pensioners outnumbering male pensioners two to one. North Norfolk, oft-times referred to as "Costa Geriatrica," houses one of the highest concentrations of elderly incomers.

Norfolk is among the top five of the most-visited counties, and Norwich is said to attract 650,000 trippers a year. In 1988 it was calculated that 7,500,000 "nights" were spent in Yarmouth, making it the third most popular seaside resort after Blackpool and Bournemouth.

The county does not possess an inch of motorway, and yet car ownership has grown faster here than almost anywhere else. In 1987, British Road Statistics said ownership was 353 per thousand population against a national average of 314; and the grandly named Office of Population Censuses and Surveys said over 68 per cent of households had one or two cars. At the same time, 2.7 per cent of households had no bath or shower, and 3.6 per cent no inside loo.

To sum up, research and statistics seem to suggest that Norfolk people are generally honest, mostly patriotic, somewhat tight-lipped and ever-so-slightly prudish; while other reported trends suggest that if you are a teeny bit inclined to reticence, prefer the company of women to men and older people to children, yearn for a sparsely populated yet fast growing region, spend less than the national average on booze, baccy, clothing and footwear, have a nest-egg for a rainy day, and look forward to a church wedding, then at the moment this is the place for you.

A crowded prom underlines the fact that Norfolk is among the top five most visited counties, with Great Yarmouth heading the popularity list.

2: The Environment

Research points to there having been a regional warm period be tween AD1000 and 1300 followed by a deteriorating climate (floods, storms), severe winters between 1430 and 1440, lots of snow and bitter winters in the 17th century, and a warm period beginning in the 1930s which continued until just after world war two.

Here are some other snippets of weather data. WIND: The gale of October, 1987, was one of the worst in memory. Another big wind on January 2, 1976, shattered a window at the Norwich Weather Centre and sent papers billowing across the room. A straight wind gust of 108mph was recorded at Cromer. COLD: An air temperature of minus 4degF was logged at Loddon in January, 1985, while minus 1.5degF was recorded at Santon Downham on January 23, 1963. SNOW: In 1975 snow fell during the first week of June. Snowiest year in recent decades was 1963, when there was snow on the ground for 64 days at Santon Downham. RAIN: In 1972, 4.5in of rain fell in two hours at Costessey; but over seven inches is said to have fallen at Brundall on August 26, 1912. DRY YEAR: Only 10.5in of rain fell at Outwell in 1921. HEAT: A temperate of 97.1degF was recorded at Hillington on August 9, 1911, a year which produced over 2000 hours of sunshine in some places. There have also been lots of weather oddities over the years. In 1950, ash from Canadian forest fires turned the sun "blue," and there have been a number of reports of Sahara "ash" giving parked cars a dusty covering. In 1984 the "ash" fell as a reddish brown rain.

An earthquake in 1994 measuring between 3.5 and 4 on the Richter scale, centered on the Necton and Swaffham area, was felt as far away as Nottingham and was Norfolk's biggest for over 100 years. Other recorded discernible county rumbles have included those of 1165, 1199, 1490, 1757, 1884 (centered on Colchester) and 1931, when the epicentre was Dogger Bank in the North Sea. Norfolk has evidently felt about 20 quakes in the last 200 years.

Norfolk covers about 2072 square miles, has over 700 villages and about 90 miles of coastline. In one way it is shrinking. It was estimated some time ago that about two acres (roughly, the size of a football pitch) is nibbled away each week by mineral extraction operations. The sea bed is also disappearing. In 1984 one firm brought ashore more than 270,000 tonnes of dredged aggregate to help build Yarmouth's western bypass.

There is said to be only one place where you can leave or enter Norfolk without crossing water, and that is by the B1113 at Redgrave Common where the road prevents the county from becoming an "island." Reason is that the source of the Little Ouse river is on the west side of the road and the source of the Waveney on the east.

"Very flat, Norfolk," is a theatrical (Noel Coward) assertion disputed by most walkers and cyclists. Norfolk merely has little hills. According to The Guinness UK Data Book (1992) its highest spot above sea level, at 335ft, is Sandy Lane, east of Sheringham. This is worrying. Some years ago the Ordnance Survey told me the highest spot, at 346ft, was near Roman Camp (which is not Roman) at East Runton. Either way, it is the lowest county highspot in the country. But what, I wonder, happened to the other 11ft? Incidentally, other claimants for Norfolk's highest spot over the years have included Piggs Grave, near Melton Constable, East Beckham and Aylmerton.

Stow Bardolph Fen, at minus 3ft, is said to be the lowest place in Norfolk. But Ordnance Survey explained some time ago that the lowest "hard point" was actually on the road by Turf Fen Farm in Methwold Fen. Spot height there had a value of minus one metre relative to OS datum.

Much of Norfolk's undulating landscape and river patterns were shaped during the last Ice Age. Hunstanton's cliffs include some of the oldest rocks in the county, dating from between 115 and 90 million years. The chalk ridge crossing the north-west of the area is five to 10 miles wide and 300 metres thick in places. Even water levels in some Breckland meres are controlled by underground chalk aquifers which occasionally present an 18-month time lag between heavy rain and high water levels.

Keen walkers will be familiar with the Great Eastern Pingo Trail, which takes in part of the old Great Eastern Railway trackbed near Stow Bedon. Pingos are shallow ponds or depressions created 20,000 years ago when melting lenses of ice carved small craters. There are also lots of pits, wells, ponds and meres in the county. Diss Mere is thought to be one of the deepest natural lakes in England. By the way, there were minor uprisings in Stanhoe and Massingham some years ago when the EDP mentioned their local ponds. In both cases, residents demanded retention of the word pit.

Ness Point at Lowestoft (Suffolk) is the country's most easterly point. Hunstanton, which faces west, is one of the country's few resorts to have a full frontal view of each day's sunset. The coastline from Holme next Sea to Sheringham faces an even more exposed view. In theory, winds can reach here undiluted all the way from Spitzbergen, Greenland, or the Arctic Circle.

About 50,000 hectares of Norfolk come within the jurisdiction of the Broads Authority, the Ministry of Defence and the Forestry Commission, or are listed as sites of special scientific interest or nature reserves. Of the remainder, arable land and built-up areas account for 82 per cent. Only 11 per cent is described as natural habitat.

Parts of Norwich are built on chalk, and tunnels and workings were exploited from the 11th or 12th centuries through to the 20th century. When an extensive network of tunnels was rediscovered in Earlham Road in 1823 they were turned into a public attraction. Coloured lights were installed and the chambers given such florid names as Bacchus Street, Royal Arch and Temple Cross. Despite this, Victorian Catholics built their new church (and later, cathedral) right on the edge of the area. The city's largest known cavern, at Eaton, is 17ft high and 15ft wide, and is a favourite haunt of bats. In recent years, heavy traffic and weakening structures have caused several collapses. Lest others take too much delight in Norwich's discomfort, it should be remembered that King's Lynn is built on mud and Yarmouth on sand and gravel.

Oil, coal and gas exploration has been a game played by prospectors for decades. In 1914, oil-bearing shales were seen as a possible source of paraffin, but high sulphur content proved a fatal stumbling block. In the 1920s oilmen thought they had struck black gold when oily deposits were seen floating down the river Puny (yes, Puny) at Setch, near King's Lynn. Workers arrived, a shanty town appeared, and the locality was extensively

Part of the old sea bank near Terrington, now landlocked in the fens.

drilled. Again, the product was too expensive to process. The hunt for coal has also taken in extensive blocks of the county. Syderstone, East Ruston, Potter Heigham, Saxthorpe and Irstead have been search areas, and in 1986 exploration licences covered the northern half of Norwich as far out as Coltishall, Aylsham, Hindolveston and Honingham, and land in Happisburgh, Acle and around Yarmouth.

Norfolk's portion of the North Sea is about 8000 years old. Before that, it was linked to the Continent by an area of forest, swamp and pools. Rising sea levels brought gradual inundation, but the remains of some of the ancient forests can still be seen at low tide on the beach at Holme, Thornham and Titchwell in the shape of flaky pieces of what looks like moist, black peat.

The parting of the waves - the division of longshore drift (the movement of beach material) - occurs near Sheringham. To the west (roughly, Hunstanton to Salthouse) the sea is leaving the coast and silt is gaining ground. East, from Weybourne to Southwold and beyond, the sea is eating into coast and cliff.

Sea defence work has been costly, complex and long standing. Near Terrington and Clenchwarton is a sea defence barrier, known misleadingly as Roman Bank, which gave added protection before the draining of the fens. It is thought to date from the early Medieval period. At Yarmouth during the 11th to 16th centuries sea access changed many times because of fluctuating levels, drainage, silting and storms. In 1567 the present Haven mouth was created. Funds were raised by public lottery, thought to be the first ever such event. More recently, beaches had to be swept by a bomb disposal unit before work was allowed to begin on a new sea wall near Winterton. Another problem encountered by the construction team was the discovery of the buried channel of the Hundred stream, former outfall of the Broads' system, which had become blocked off from the sea.

Much of the sea bed is unexplored, but a sub-aqua enthusiast once told me he had visited Church Rock, off Cromer, finding a section of flint wall, and the wreck of the Amberley, which sank off Wells in 1973. Prettiest wreck he had seen was the Rosalie, off Weybourne, then covered with white and pink sea anemones. He had also explored the Cromer-Holt chalk ridge, which extended for a short distance along the sea bed, and visited chalk caves off Sheringham. And some years ago another diver reported that a hasty visit to the delivery end of one local sewage pipe produced the spectacle of "a Sargasso Sea of contraceptives" waving on the seabed.

Jet fighter pilots skimming the Wash at 200ft towards RAF Holbeach (Holbeach Marsh) firing range sometimes use as a visual marker "The Plug," two miles north of the Nene mouth. It is a circular man-made island, also known as Rabbit Island, which from the air, as I can vouch, does look like a giant bath plughole. It comprises inner and outer banks to contain a lagoon and was built in the 1970s of stone, slag and gravel, and topsoil from King's Lynn where it had been washed off sugar beet at the local processing factory. Officially, it was an offshore study into the feasibility of water storage. Unofficially, the aim of the project is thought to have been to test the idea of siting nuclear power stations on offshore islands. The schemes sank.

Norfolk's wetlands are affected by rainfall, evaporation, seepage, springs, the water table, boreholes and drainage. The Heacham river between Sedgeford and Fring - or the bit that crosses the Peddars Way - often disappears during the summer or is reduced to puddle proportions. Apparently it all depends on the volume of rain the previous autumn. Some rivers, however, are getting wider by 4ft or so every 10 years. Boat wash and bank erosion are two reasons.

Water names are interesting. My favourite is the tiny "river" Puny, near Setch. But it is a complicated subject as brooks, becks and burns have to be considered, too. Such as Scarrow Beck (near Erpingham), Wades Beck (Thursford), Goose Beck (Burnham Market), Landspring Beck (Haddiscoe), and Dyke Beck (Wymondham). Then there are stretches of water like Seamere (Hingham) and Craymere or Crymer (Briston). Lenwade echoes a crossing point. Some river names are thought to have been invented by historians, or are back formations, like Ingol (Ingoldisthorpe), Thet (Thetford), Ant (Antingham), Nar (Narford) and Chet (Chedgrave). The Ouse may be one of the oldest river names in the area. But that still leaves the Tiffey, Wissey, Erne, Stoke, Stiffkey, Wensum and Bure. To mention but a few. And what of perhaps the most common name of them all, Blackwater? One thought is that it may have had something to do with crossing points, fords, and disturbed water.

The disappearing Heacham river, spotted at Fring Cross on the Peddars Way.

Welney is built along the old course of the river Cam. Outwell is said to have the largest "village green" in England because it is built on both sides of what was once the home of the

Water over water, at the Mullicourt Aqueduct, near Outwell.

river which divided Cambridgeshire from Norfolk. The waterway was dry by 1794 and later re-dug as a canal, but the canal was abandoned in 1926 and closed in 1939.

There are lots of "ford" place-names in Norfolk. And there were once mounted guides for travellers crossing the old Wellstream estuary from Cross Keys (Norfolk) to Long Sutton, on the far bank in Lincolnshire. One of them was Charles Wigglesworth, "late of Sutton Bridge, corn merchant and guide, Long Sutton Wash," whose tombstone in Long Sutton churchyard was dated 1840.

Mullicourt Aqueduct near Outwell carries water over water - the Well Creek over the Middle Level. But there are lots of other ways to cross water. One is by ferry. West Lynn ferry once carried Walsingham pilgrims. Gorleston ferry claims to have been running since the time of King John, and Reedham, Norfolk's only vehicle-carrying ferry, reckons it has been in business for 300 years.

The 23,000 acres of the Stanford Battle Area are under military "protection." About 13,500 acres of this army training ground are designated as sites of special scientific interest. Some sections have never been ploughed and some have not been ploughed since the 1850s. The evacuation of the Battle Area villages early in world war two represented one of the last enforced mass evictions of Norfolk people from their homes. Frog Hill, a 175ft chalk ridge, is a rare example of traditional Breckland heath. Indeed, the whole place is a sort of time capsule, said to contain over 600 flower and plant species, 330 moth species, 28 types of butterfly, and 137 bird and 26 mammal species. It is also home to several thousand grazing ewes. In spring, wild fruit trees and flowers mark the sites of former household gardens, and stone curlew and red deer haunt the margins of the firing ranges.

Thetford Forest Park embraces 80 square miles of largely conifer plantations - the largest lowland forest in Britain. Holkham nature reserve, which embraces 10,000 acres of marsh, dune and mudflat along nine miles of coast, is the largest reserve in England. Norfolk's smallest nature reserve is a single tree - the Hethel Thorn. The enclosed "reserve" covers a mere 140 square yards, and some of the trunk has died. But it clings to life. The thorn, near Hethel church, is thought to be East Anglia's oldest living example of crataegus monogyna, and was once known as the Witch of Hethel. The first Sir Thomas Beevor claimed to have a 13th century document referring to it as a boundary tree, and it may also have been a meeting place during the insurrection of peasants during the reign of King John.

Tyrrels Wood, a Woodland Trust reserve, two miles south of Long Stratton, is thought to date to the last Ice Age. Shelfanger meadows, near Diss, are considered one of the most important areas of unimproved grassland in Norfolk. The name of Wayland Wood, near Watton, derives from Old Norse for a grove, or sacred grove.

There are thought to be about 11,000 acres of commons or village greens in Norfolk, many now in private hands. Among the best known commons are New Buckenham, Mulbarton, West Winch, Barnham, Swardeston, Foulden and Roydon, near King's Lynn. In the 1960s about 450 commons were submitted to local authorities for registration. Following several years of legal work, however, the actual number registered was 345.

Redgrave and Lopham Fen is the only known habitat of Britain's biggest and rarest spider, the great raft spider, or dolomedes plantarius. Raft spiders walk on water and stalk damsel flies and pond skaters. The area is particularly sensitive to water level fluctuations, and although pools have been excavated to help them, their continued existence remains in the balance. One of Britain's smallest and rarest spiders, thought to be extinct for 70 years, was found in 1991 in a sedge-bed at Catfield Fen. The single specimen, the size of a matchhead, was identified as a male of the robertus insignis species. Flordon Common is thought to be the final English refuge of the miniscule narrow-mouthed moss or whorl snail, the shell of which whorls to the left. This sets it royally apart from ordinary right-whorling snails.

Just outside Wymondham is The Lizard, a stretch of water meadow apparently given to the town over 350 years ago. Bitter rows over rights of way and use have bubbled to the surface regularly over the years. In 1912 the EDP, reporting yet another dispute, claimed the documents relating to the land gift had been destroyed in the town fire of 1615. There were other disputes over pasturage, over the siting of a golf club, and more recently over the line of Wymondham's newest bypass. The Lizard is thought to have taken its name from a Lazar or plague house.

Norfolk's smallest nature reserve, the Hethel Thorn, near Hethel church.

It was once calculated that the county had lost 70 plant species, and that a further 30 species were in danger. This explains why tight security surrounded a site which supported the rare military orchid, orchis militaris, in a forest plantation a few miles from Thetford. The last time I visited it, this well disguised Suffolk Trust for Conservation site was open for one day a year. There were no signposts and the site was not advertised. The pink or purple orchids thrived on the grassy bottom of a depression among the trees, and the area was secured by a high fence fringed with barbed wire, and a padlocked gate. Special wooden walkways enabled visitors to walk above, but not on, the precious plants.

This is the oak tree at Dilham, not far from the church, which produced black banded acorns.

Another rare species, the fingered speedwell, clung to existence on the edge of the Cloverfields housing estate at Thetford. Yet another, the smooth rupturewort, or herniaria glabra, was spotted growing in a rain gutter, also at Thetford.

Some plants are becoming more plentiful. Giant hogweed is one, having arrived in the county only a decade or so ago. Himalayan balsam (policeman's helmet) is another. Brought to this country by Victorian gardeners it can now be found in the Wensum Valley and elsewhere. Australian swamp stonecrop (or New Zealand pygmy weed) has reached Hickling, while Japanese knotweed also has a footing in the Wensum Valley.

On the other hand, rosebay willowherb's rise from scarcity took 150 years. Like the poppy, it thrives in areas of human activity and disturbance. The surfaces of newly-made railway embankments in mid-Norfolk in the 1880s gave the plant its chance, and the ravages of two world wars encouraged its spread. Now it helps to give Breckland its lovely pink or purplish summer tinge.

The East Anglian or smooth-leaved elm is a traditional landscape element, but the tree comes in many varieties, sometimes with leaves peculiar to a single parish. In the 1970s some 172,000 elms were wiped out by Dutch elm disease. Local elms were also devastated 3500 years ago, though the reason is uncertain.

Many of Norfolk's oaks are past their prime, stag-headed and ivy-todded. One oak at South Walsham, the King Oak, was said locally to have been 900 years old. Kett's Oak, between Wymondham and Hethersett, was said to have been one of the gathering points for Robert Kett's followers during the uprising of 1549. In 1990, acorns from this tree were collected and propagated at the Easton Agricultural College, and in 1992 a dozen were re-planted in an effort to keep its history alive.

Hitler's Oak, at How Hill, was presented by the Hitler administration and planted in 1936 to commemorate a gold medal won by the six-metre yacht Lalage, of the Royal Corinthian Yacht Club, during the Olympic sailing events in Kiel. Lalage's helmsman was Christopher Boardman, whose father lived at How Hill at the time. Oddly, a world war two German raider discarded a stick of bombs in the vicinity, and one of them exploded sufficiently close to spray the garden with shrapnel. Tree and house survived.

The Dilham Oak, a common pendunculate, used to produce black-banded acorns, perhaps the only tree in the county to have done so. When I visited the site near Dilham church some years ago it was the eighth tree down the line from the road junction. But time and gales may have taken their toll. Little is known of the tree's history aside from the fact that it was well grown in 1872, and that in 1912 it was judged to be about 70 years' old.

About 20 per cent of Norfolk's mammal species are introduced, accidently or deliberately. Even the domestic cat and the house mouse are immigrants. Not even the rabbit is thought to be native. As for the pheasant, it was originally Oriental and is known to have been in the British Isles before 1058. Another famous introduction is the Canada goose, which probably arrived through the Wretham and Holkham parks. A flock is a familiar sight at Holkham during the moult migration and they clearly see Holkham as an ancestral home. Influences on all these creatures have included ships, pet shops, landowners, zoos and estates. Chinese water deer, muntjac, red, roe and Sika deer may have emanated from such sources. Fallow deer were reputedly brought in by the Romans, along with edible frogs.

An American rodent called the coypu became a plague in the 1950s and 60s when local populations were estimated at 200,000, the highest in the world. Introduced in 1929 for nutria fur, which enjoyed brief popularity, some 50 farms sprang up in the region. By 1940 most had closed and many animals had escaped. In 1948 the EDP recorded a "delightful" scene at Cringleford of children watching a pair of coypus playing in the river. But they were a growing nuisance, gnawing root crops and plants and damaging river banks. In 1965, the work of containing the numbers was taken over by Coypu Control, and in 1977 alone 11,800 were trapped and killed. By 1981 the population was down to 10,000, and in 1988 it was thought the very last one had been killed on the banks of the Ouse near St Neots. A few weeks later a male was trapped near Peterborough.

Escaped exotics occasionally make news. Capybara have been known to enjoy moments of freedom in the Kilverstone area. Some years ago racoon sightings were reported near Kelling, and in 1987 a leopard was said to have been spotted padding along a road between Eccles and Lessingham. Three pairs of wallabies fled a zoo at Northrepps in the 1850s. It is known they died, but wallaby-sighting stories have persisted over the years. Perhaps, somewhere, there is a secret wallaby farm. At the time of writing a "puma-like" creature was also on the run having been spotted variously at Skeyton, Reepham, Alderford, Tunstead, Hoveton, Tacolneston, Hapton and Forncett St Peter.

The Wash and Norfolk's coastal areas embrace a cat's cradle of bird migration routes, and passing birds of all kinds regularly use offshore rigs as resting places. In 1989 a parakeet dropped in for lunch on the Shell Esso Leman Foxtrot platform, 60 miles offshore. That same year the owners of South Pier, Lowestoft, built an artificial cliff to provide a new home for kittiwakes after their old nesting ground had been demolished. Three years earlier, a commuting heron crashlanded on the Eight Alpha North Sea gas platform, 25 miles off Grimsby. Adopted by the crew of the rig ship Stirling Tern, it was taken to Yarmouth and thence to a bird clinic. Though tired and thin, it duly recovered.

A homing pigeon was once the hero of a search and rescue mission off the Norfolk coast. In 1917 a Royal Naval Air Service seaplane went to rescue the crew of a ditched DeHaviland 4 off Yarmouth. But the seaplane broke down, so the crew turned to HM Pigeon number NVRP/17/16331. It flew to shore, the message was found, and six lives were saved. When 16331 died it was not forgotten. Instead, it was stuffed and still resides, I am told, at the RAF Museum at Hendon.

Incidentally, there are pigeon lofts owned by the Sandringham Royal Estate, and an official Keeper of the Queen's Flight. And Cetti's warblers are said to have developed regional song, or dialect. As for Sheringham's low-lying beaches, they are said to attract more Alpine swifts that anywhere else in the country.

Chickens have adventures, too. I recall one living wild for at least a couple of years amid the conifers at Bridgham picnic area. A stray cockerel, thought to have escaped from Swaffham market, took up residence for a couple of years in Orchard Place. In 1987 a cockerel subsequently named Ross was rescued from the side of a road at Gillingham to become the office pet of an engineering firm at Mettingham (Suffolk), near Bungay.

Flying sheep? A flying flock, anyway. They belong to Norfolk Naturalists' Trust and are kept occupied by being moved around the county, from one protected site to another, to nibble coarse vegetation and help keep patches of heathland, common and old grassland in good shape. The Shetland sheep even spawned a natty tee-shirt emblem: the Flying Flock.

Every year since about 1976 a 200lb seal has deserted its Norfolk coastal haunts for a winter trip in the Broads. In 1994 it turned up in the river Wensum in the middle of Norwich for a short visit. Over the years, and particularly in Rockland Broad, it has proved to be a much better pike fisher than local anglers.

A few years ago a potential champion pike was found dead in the river at Thurne. It was over 50in long with a girth of 28in, and was thought to be over 20 years' old. It may have weighed 55lb when alive.

In the 1950s a Meteor jet crashed near the railway lines at Trowse, leaving a crater which duly filled with water. Ten years or so later someone stocked it with fish and in 1980, when British Rail began to build its huge rolling stock cleaning depot, 16 fat carp were rescued before the crater was filled in. Eleven were put into another pond, but a passing heron got them within days. The five remaining veterans were given a place of honour in a special tank in the amenity block of the new complex.

Common frogs sometimes undergo a temporary colour change during the breeding season, and the late, much-loved naturalist E A Ellis once recalled he has seen magenta and yellow females. In 1983 an orange frog was reported in a garden at Sprowston. Retired mole-catcher Lester Farman, of Thurton, said in 1994 that in his 50-year career, during which he had caught 40,000 moles, he could remember some which were white, spotted, dark green and even golden coloured.

Providing one of the few British sightings of Nathusius' pipistrelle bats, a stowaway was landed at Yarmouth from a container ship in 1984. It was placed in a jam jar and returned alive to Holland as an "illegal immigrant."

Some years ago a puss named Abigail, of Thorpe, was rescued after spending six weeks entombed under floorboards. She disappeared when workmen were fixing the floor of an empty house. Six weeks' later the new owner heard mewing. A board was lifted and Abigail appeared, having evidently survived on spiders, the odd mouse, and condensation on water pipes.

In 1984, Tickle, a Jack Russell from Attlebridge, disappeared shortly after producing a litter of puppies. Nineteen days later Tickle's owners were in the garden when they heard muffled barking from under ground at the top of a nearby 15ft high road embankment. The soil was carefully dug and there, a few inches below the surface, weak and distressed, was Tickle. It seems she had become trapped in a rabbit hole and had spent the next 19 days tunnelling 15ft to within inches of the top of the bank.

It was reported in 1986 that a dog cocked its leg against a traffic light in Thorpe. Alas, a short circuit sent it spinning away and all the lights went out at the Thunder Lane/St William's Way junction. The dog was last seen retreating towards nearby trees.

On August 10, 1810, the famous trotting stallion Marshland Shales trotted 17 miles in 56 minutes carrying 12st 2lb. Marshland Shales was afterwards sold at a King's Lynn auction for a little over £300.

In 1987 a tortoise named Ali Pasha died of a cold. His age was unknown, but he had lived in Lowestoft for 72 years. Ali was said to have been picked up on a beach in Gallipoli on April 26, 1915, by Henry Friston, who had gone ashore with a landing party from HMS Implaccable. Ali was enlisted as ship's mascot and eventually brought back to Lowestoft. When the frigate HMS Brave anchored off Lowestoft in 1986 Ali Pasha was taken on a special sea trip to meet the Navy once again.

At the time of writing measures were being taken to protect the 600,000-year-old remains of an elephant found in the cliffs at West Runton. Only partially excavated, the fossil elephant, in its prime, would have stood 13ft 4in at the shoulder, or twice the size of the modern African elephant. It was the oldest and largest fossil elephant skeleton found in Britain.

3: Marking out the Space

Viewed from 500 miles, or more precisely from Landsat 5 satellite images, the region's most immediately recognisible man made ob jects are the two parallel Bedford rivers in the Fens and the Washes between. On some Landsat 5 slides Thetford's pine forests and a couple of Roman roads - the Peddars Way, and near Holkham - are also plain to see.

In 1994 astronauts orbiting 133 miles above the earth in a Nasa spacecraft aimed a radar beam at a small triangular reflector in a field at Feltwell. It was all part of a plan to map the face of the earth and monitor environmental change, the information fed down in this case being on the state of Thetford Forest, local crops and groundwater levels.

A few years ago I visited a 325ft tower not far from Poringland and only a mile or two from a cluster of more mysterious looking clones at Upper Stoke's post office relay station. The single mast at Shotesham, a sort of radio lighthouse, was part of the Racal-Decca Navigator system. It had a range of about 300 miles and transmitted signals which pilots and sailors used to plot their position on charts over-printed with coloured lines. The system was first tested in the 1940s, and 30 years or so later there were more than 50 chains all over the globe, each chain consisting of a "master" and three "slave" stations - red, purple and green. Master was in Hertfordshire, green slave in Sussex and purple slave in Oxfordshire. Red slave of Shotesham had transmitted its solitary note unbroken, apart from servicing time, since 1947.

The world's most famous invisible line, the Greenwich zero Meridian line, merely clips the region, most accessibly, perhaps, on the A151 at Wignall's Gate, Holbeach (Lincolnshire). But in August, 1987, according to newspaper reports, a number of planets were aligned in a way predicted in ancient South American and Hopi Indian writings relating to the birth of a new millenium. The dates August 16-17 have significance for the Hopi who, it was said, participated in ritual dances to light up two leylines which crisscrossed the world. One of them was the St Michael Dragon Line, said to pass through Stoke Holy Cross.

The most famous modern parallel lines in Norfolk are probably those of the Acle New Road (the Straight), built in 1831, and the railway line between Acle and Yarmouth, built a few years later. For six miles road and line run side by side across the flat marsh. Incidentally, Norwich jurisdiction on the river Yare extends over 15 miles downstream to Hardley Cross, a monument put in place by Norwich in 1543 on the south bank of the Yare beside the entrance to the river Chet. Traditionally, the mayors of Norwich and Yarmouth travelled by water to meet there.

Norfolk had about two dozen concrete Ordnance Survey triangulation points which for 60 years enabled map-makers and surveyors plot precise locations. In 1993, however, the OS decided the points were redundant and put them up for "adoption" by members of the public. Among the best known trig points is one on the Peddars Way at Shepherd's Bush, near Castle Acre, and another on the top of Beeston Hill, Sheringham.

The county's tallest landmark was thought to be the 360ft chimney of Yarmouth's old power station, which beat Norwich cathedral spire for height by about 45ft. The power station closed in 1985, and at the time of writing there were plans to demolish the chimney.

Earliest known printed copy of a British town plan is that of Norwich, in 1559, by physician and astrologer William Cunningham. However, once you start to put things on maps the real problems begin. Lines and boundaries create division. In this particular "war" parts of Fenland have always been in the front line. One reason is that many boundaries were based on rivers and river banks. Now some of the rivers have disappeared or moved.

Welney evolved in the Middle Ages by the old course of the river Cam. Over the centuries the Cam built up levees of silt. Then it dried out and became a roddon (the silt bed left standing proud after surrounding land levels had fallen). Walsoken is barely indistinguishable from Wisbech (Cambridgeshire), yet it is divided by the Cambridgeshire-Norfolk border. Emneth is another flashpoint, while Outwell and Upwell have plagued Boundary Commissioners for decades. Difficulties arose here because the Well Creek, the old course of the river, is the county dividing line and because the villages developed on both banks. In the 1950s it was gleefully pointed out in one newspaper that Outwell and Upwell each had parish councils; that both churches, though in Norfolk, were in the Isle of Ely diocese; that Upwell school, in Norfolk, came under the jurisdiction of the Isle; that the Isle policeman at Upwell had to cycle through Norfolk to visit the nearby village of Christchurch; that Upwell's main street was in Norfolk and the Isle of Ely; and that the postal address for both was Wisbech, Cambridgeshire.

The confusion continues. At the time of writing there are proposals to amend Norfolk's European parliamentary boundaries which would include "moving" 78,000 Norfolk people in the Watton, Swaffham, Downham Market, Thetford and Attleborough areas into a new Euro seat to be called Suffolk and South West Norfolk. Even more chilling are other proposals to do away with Norfolk County Council, thus putting the name Norfolk at risk and perhaps into some sort of Middlesex or Rutland-type limbo. All these boundaries, of course, are quite different again from diocesan, district, heath, water and parliamentary boundaries.

One fine example of boundary confusion was an inn at Tydd Gote which, because of a kink in the Lincolnshire and Cambridgeshire boundary, sat astride the division. The pub had two sets of opening times, two justices' licences, and darts players who threw their darts in Cambs at a dartboard hanging in Lincs. Such divisions still exist. A

At Upwell, as at other places in the Fens, building took place on both sides of the county line, in this case the Well Creek.

number of houses in Margetson Avenue, Thorpe, are in Broadland and the City local authority areas.

Talking of parliamentary boundaries, Yarmouth, King's Lynn, Norwich and Thetford and Castle Rising were at one time all boroughs. Indeed, Castle Rising - which returned two MPs, the same as Norwich and as many as any town or city in the land, London excepted - was not demoted to parish status until 1835.

Hoveton was handicapped for years because many people thought it was Wroxham. The river Bure is the boundary, with the bridge sort of half-and-half. But the problem arose when the site for the railway station for Wroxham, on the Norwich side of the river, was belatedly switched to the Hoveton side because of technical difficulties. The station signs were already painted, however, and the name remained. Thus Hoveton businesses, having goods delivered by rail, had to give their station address as Wroxham. In 1987 Hoveton finally persuaded British Rail to change the name of the station to Hoveton & Wroxham, but it had to pay £720 to get its name back.

Sometimes it is necessary to try to remember where boundaries are. Each Rogation Sunday choirboys from St Peter Mancroft, Norwich, beat the bounds of the parish, during which they progress to the Coach and Horses pub in Bethel Street - built on the boundary - where the gathering enjoy fruit juice drinks and "bumping" the youngest choirboy.

Norfolk's place-name archive is not deposited locally but at Uppsala University, Sweden. The reason is that following the death of Dr O K Schram the English Placename Society decided the data needed organising into an archive. Uppsala was chosen because of the strong Scandinavian element in many Norfolk names and because it would be in the care of Dr Karl Inge Sandred, who had himself researched many of Norfolk's Scandinavian names.

Among the oldest local names and place-names are thought to be Ouse, Trunch, North and South Creake, Brancaster, Lynn, and possibly Eccles. Some interpretations fire the imagination. Walcot can be translated as serf's cottage and Ashmanhaugh as a pirates' enclosure. Other possibilities include Stiffkey (tree stump island), Sharrington (dung or muddy enclosure), Tivetshall (lapwings' nook), Cromer (crow's pond), Wiveton (wife's enclosure), Belaugh (funeral pyre enclosure), Glandford (merriment ford, ie sports), Harpley (harp player's clearing) and Weybourne (felons' stream, where criminals were drowned). California, near Yarmouth, is said to have been so named after the discovery of treasure trove on the beach at the time of the American Gold Rush which began in 1848/49.

Beware of drawing easy conclusions. Wicklewood may mean "wych elm wood," but it could have been a single elm in a forest of oak. Even so, Long Stratton does suggest a Roman road, Eccles could relate to an early church, and Brettenham may mean "the Briton." In fact there are plenty of names to keep you guessing. Among my favourites, including some field and plantation names, are or were: Quarles, Ivy Todd, Daffy Green, Hulver Street, Foxhole, Loddon Ingloss, Elmersdale, Squalham, Kenwick, Crackthorn Corner, Smoker's Hole, Puddledock, Hills and Holes, High Wrong Corner, Summerpit Bottom, Old Middlegouch, Severals, Queach, The Nab, Lobb's Valley, Nogdam End, Short Whins, Stowe Ollands, Fustyweed, Skipping Block, Gillows Willows, Garlic Street, Hell Hole, The Thicks, Eel's Foot, Reydon Smear, Sot's Hole, Emorsgate, Cat's Bottom, The Sincks, Devil's Bottom, Oby, Cess and Gristlewood.

Little Snoring once wrote to a Sunday newspaper chiding it for a TV advertisement which suggested the village was a sleepy place. It argued that as the newspaper was using the village's name it ought to pay for the privilege. The result was a £100 cheque for the village hall and playing field fund. As for Nowhere, a newspaper item by the author a few years ago elicited information about six or seven such places in the area including Repps, Acle, West Caister, Great Witchingham, Wiveton, Wenhaston and Wereham. Some seemed to have been scraps of land at places where parish boundaries met. A parish walk at Reepham, incidentally, took strollers to Nowhere and World's End!

My very favourite Norfolk place-name is Swacking Cuckoo, a quarter of a mile east of the A148 and south of the railway cutting where the Norwich to Cromer line crosses the Holt-Cromer road. It is a small area of a few houses and woods.

Even sandbanks are interesting. Scroby Sands, once claimed by Yarmouth and named Yarmouth Island, may be a derivation of Scratby. Silver Pits got its name because of rich catches. But what of Tea Kettle Hole, Ribs and Trucks Pit, Botney Gut, Brown Ridges and Monkey Bank? And who was Smith of Smith's Knoll, or the Bob Hall who gave his name to a sandbank off Wells? Or Ferrier and Daseley banks in the Wash? Incidentally, did you know there is a Hospital on Dogger Bank where fishermen believe the sick fish go?

Farm names tend to come in categories. There is the land type category (Sandy Farm, Marsh, Chalk); the descriptive (Lower Farm, Crossways, Moat, High); the place-name (Choseley); the commemorative (Waterloo, Balaclava, Cuidad Rodrigo); the comforting (Home); and the remote (America, Botany Bay, North Pole). Injun Farm may be derived from engine (ie, steam engine). Goodness knows the story behind Starknaked Farm, though.

Every parish had its quota of field names. Reflections of disgust seem to include Poverty Piece, Starve Cow, Labour in Vain, Sourdale and Misery. Pudding Norton had Polly Breck, Pewdy Pond and Flagmore. Blo Norton had Great Watchcocks and Knives. Dumpling Green, near Dereham, had Duffews (dove house), Clerkes Crowches (clerk's cross) and Sirricks Trumpasses. Gift lands might be named Lord's Pightle, Parson's Piece or Church Meadow, and the poor might benefit from Charity Lands, Poor Man's Piece or The Dole. Sermon Meadow provided income for an annual sermon on the virtue of the benefactor.

Other odd fieldnames include Smee or Smeath (open land, or an open level area); Spong (often a narrow strip, or wet and boggy); Wong or Wang (area of unenclosed parish land, sometimes low lying, damp or wet); and Bullymung (including crops such as peas, oats, vetches, or mixed meal for poultry or pigs). Pightle (in Norfolk, a small field enclosed by a hedge) is in use in various forms all over Britain and parts of the USA.

A field once gave its name to a telephone exchange - the Pangle, a piece of charity land at Wereham, near Stoke Ferry. In 1980 the number range on the Stoke Ferry exchange was full and the equipment due to be replaced. As a temporary measure during conversion two extra racks were added to the exchange, with their own code. The racks were named Pangle, after the nearby field. It had a brief curiousity value before the Pangle numbers were finally merged with Stoke Ferry again.

Who was the constable, I wonder, at Policeman's Loke, Hardingham?

In the 1930s much of the land in Beach Road, Snettisham, was owned by a Dr Learoyd, of Heacham, who laid out a camp site and encouraged Scout troops from the poorer areas of London to visit. The site was named Diglea. After the war most of the Diglea site was sold, though three acres were retained to become the local troop's campsite. It was then re-named Jimmy's Field, in memory of Jimmy Otway, an orphan, who joined the Scout troop and who lost his life in world war two when his Merchant Navy ship was torpedoed.

Norfolk County Council maintains 5660 miles of "county" roads and looks after a further 600 or so miles of trunk roads for the Department of Transport. About 600 miles of road are resurfaced in an average year. There are also about 40,000 street and road lighting columns in the county. Norfolk also has over 3000 miles of footpaths and bridleways. The construction of Norwich's southern bypass, opened in 1992, involved the excavation of over 2 million cubic metres of earthworks, while 1.5 million tonnes of material was used in the embankments.

Some roads retain their names for a long time. Ferrygate, which runs from the river Thurne into Martham, was called Feriegate in 1292 - over 700 years ago. An early pedestrian underpass was built at Letheringsett in 1808 when the main road was diverted. The tunnel enabled people to get to church more easily and also connected with a pond, dug in 1805 for brewery use, which supplied the Hall with water.

High Street is thought to have been an original reference to raised Roman roads, and later used to denote any road of importance. Smuggler's Road at Bodney may be comparatively modern despite following the line of the ancient Icknield Way. Policeman's Loke at Hardingham (in Norfolk, a loke is a lane) may echo a police house. The Bleaches, between Albion Road, Apsley Road and Regent Road in Yarmouth, was an area traditionally used by residents for hanging out their washing. O'Callaghan Place, Dereham, is named after Bill O'Callaghan, a world war two hero; Wodehouse Road, Old Hunstanton, commemorates local links with the writer P G Wodehouse; Sunsalve Ride, Toftwood, recalls the locally-bred showjumper Sunsalve which won a bronze medal at the Rome Olympics as well as carrying off the British men's and women's showjumping championships; and St Peter's Close, near a sheltered housing complex at Yaxham, ironically reflects the passage of time; but I have still to find any 19th hole along Golf Links Road at Morley. Meanwhile, a Hemsby researcher discovered that Pit Road was once called Moonshine Road, while St Mary's Close was also called Moonshine. Banish all thought of illicit stills, though. The names are thought to refer to old nightsoil emptying sites.

Not so long ago questions were asked about Maude Gray Court, off St Benedict Street, Norwich. Basically, who was Maude Gray? Newspaper readers responded with theories of a ghost, an American world war two Liberator bomber, a jazz singer and a Lowestoft drifter. They were wrong. Maude Gray was a miniature dachsund owned by a friend of the site developer. Various names for the Court had been suggested and rejected. Then someone suggested Maude Gray, who was six-years-old when the secret was revealed.

The name Shaker's Furze, near Thompson, and Shaker's Road on Wangford Warren, can also be found in the Bury St Edmunds', Woolpit, Ixworth and Ickburgh areas of Suffolk. It is a puzzle. Furze, of course, is gorse. As for Shaker, connections with boneshakers and the Shaker movement are usually ruled out. One theory is that is might relate to a "shaking" (meaning blown or shifting sand or soil) road. Another explanation is that it might refer to aspen trees or bushes, the leaves of which appear to palpitate or shake.

At the time of writing Wymondham is about to add to its uniqueness in that the town will have at least the beginnings of three main roads to Norwich - the old Norwich road, the new Norwich road, and the latest bypass, currently under construction.

A commemorative pillar dedicated to Sir Edwin Rich, dated 1675, sits in a layby beside the A11 at Morley. It commemorated a gift of money by Sir Edwin which enabled Norfolk's first stretch of turnpike, from Wymondham to Attleborough, to be built and opened in 1695.

Roadside verges on some of the county's bypasses are beginning to resemble nature reserves. Giant hogweed and lupins occasionally appear beside the Cringleford bypass, while Dereham's bypass has been cropped for hay. In 1956, turnips grew beside the Brandon to Swaffham road, surplus farm soil containing turnip seed having been spread on the verges at Ickburgh.

Mann Egerton of Norwich opened one of the first driving schools in the area and its 1919 teaching car was a vehicle with dual steering wheels. Collins the chemist in Gentleman's Walk in the city once produced a potion designed to boost confidence prior to a driving test. Reluctant to reveal the ingredients, Collins said the mixture was "nothing special." It simply contained "something" to aid nervous candidates.

One early Norfolk vehicle registration prefix was NG. In fact, NG1 was originally allocated to an Austin 7 in 1930. In the early 1970s, NG1 was on a London taxi owned by multi-millionaire Nubar Gulbenkian, while NG2, NG3 and NG4 were owned by the Government of Nigeria for their official cars in London. In 1981, EX plates were issued to new vehicles in Norfolk, and at about the time AEX had worked its way through to REX an unprecedented postbag of application forms arrived from all over the UK. Alas, SEX was not allowed to raise its ugly head. Tantalisingly, the sequence jumped to TEX.

Village signs were popularised by the Royal Family and first appeared in most of the Sandringham estate villages, including West Newton, Babingley, Flitcham, Wolferton and Shernbourne, in 1912. Eighty or so years later the tradition has spread throughout the county. A Norfolk village without its own sign is now quite rare.

This granite block from Massachusetts, now in Hingham, replaced a mounting block sent as a present from Hingham to Hingham, Mass. Good news for the carriers, no doubt.

Weybourne's tenuous link with the continent ended in 1986 when the telegraph repeater station sent its last message across the North Sea. Weybourne had been sending and receiving messages since 1858 when a 280-mile cable linked the village to the German coastal island of Borkum. In 1952 another cable was laid to the Danish port of Esbjerg, installed by the Great Northern Telegraph Company of Denmark. For years, diplomatic messages flowed through the village, one link having been between Moscow and London. News of Russia's first space flight is said to have reached Britain through Weybourne. But the links were severed, literally, on closedown when cable 901VFT was unceremoniously cut with a hacksaw. Another cable system came ashore at Cable Gap, Bacton, and ran to a repeater station in Mundesley Road, North Walsham. Other sea cables came ashore at Mundesley and Winterton.

Norfolk's first county town was Venta Icenorum (Caistor St Edmund), which at its peak was probably about the size of present-day Hingham. Newest towns, aside from Bowthorpe, are New Hunstanton, developed by Hamon Le Strange with the coming of the railway line in 1862, and Melton Constable, founded in 1881 as a railway town and built on empty land near the site of the deserted village of Burgh Parva. New Buckenham, on the other hand, is as old as the Normans.

A few years ago it was calculated that parochial charities in Norfolk probably numbered about 1700, though many were ineffective. One Breckland village was supposed to distribute 15 yards of cloth to the poor and aged on Christmas Day, and a West Norfolk village was bidden to give blankets to those of the needy who attended church regularly. A Congham charity provided £15 a year - usually spent on fruit, flowers or chocolates - for elderly patients in hospital. And bread loaves were handed out to children at Fleggburgh and Burgh St Margaret, the money coming from the rent of a piece of land known as Plough Loaf Field.

Beside the post office at Hingham is a granite block presented by the people of Hingham, Massachusetts. The stone was a replacement for an ancient mounting block sent to America in the early 1900s to commemorate folk who emigrated from Hingham, Norfolk, to Hingham, Mass, in the 17th century.

Norfolk has over 340 scheduled Ancient Monuments and over 10,000 listed buildings. Two unusual protected structures are a metal drawbridge of 1864 at Mannington Hall, and Denver Sluice, at the junction of the Great Ouse and the New Bedford, which was rebuilt by Sir John Rennie in 1834. Rennie's brickwork remains intact and constitutes Norfolk's only underwater listed building. A listed AA box in a layby off the A149 at Brancaster Staithe is one of only a few sentry-style black boxes still in working order. Over 30 years old, it is the oldest AA box in East Anglia. But mistakes can happen. In 1988, the Department of the Environment officially listed Moss Fen Lodge at Sea Palling as a 16th century house of special historical and architectural interest. Alas, it was built between 1979 and 1983 of old materials, complete with beams, bulging walls and sagging floors.

There are over 400 medieval moated sites in the county, either existing or known to have existed. Opinions differ as to why they were dug - decoration, fashion (echoing castles, for example), clay extraction, water supply, cattle pound, fish ponds, or even early Norfolk attempts to keep strangers at bay. No-one really knows.

The sites of over 200 deserved medieval villages have been logged in the county, along with over 24,000 recorded archaeological sites, including 800 windmills. Talking of villages reminds me that in 1987 Yarmouth's development control sub-committee members got into a discussion over the ugliest village in Norfolk. Some thought Belton worthy of the title while others supported Hemsby. The matter was tactfully left unresolved.

This AA box, in a layby off the A149 at Brancaster Staithe, is over 30 years old and an official listed building.

Yarmouth Tolhouse, in Middlegate Street, is the oldest civil building in the town. Built before 1362, it had been used by the Corporation since before 1552 and as a courtroom and archive. It was rebuilt in 1622 for council meetings, gutted by incendiary bombs during world war two, and used as the jail from 1261 to 1835. It was at the Tolhouse that the saintly Sarah Martin (1791-1843) of Caister did much of her caring work among the prisoners.

Caister Castle, built between 1446 and 1454 may have been the first brick-built residence in

Norfolk, aside from those built by the Romans. One of King's Lynn's earliest known domestic buildings, No 28-30 King Street, may have been occupied continuously since the latter half of the 12th century. Members of the Bedingfeld family have lived at Oxburgh Hall since it was built by their Catholic ancestors in 1482. Wymondham had an unusual number of "flying freeholds" - terraced rows where a room in one house may be over (or under) a room of the house next door.

Waxham Great Barn is the oldest in the county, dating from the late 16th century. Hales Hall Barn is probably the largest. The bulk of Norfolk's hundreds of surviving barns were built between 1750 and 1850.

Centuries ago the cygnet was a delicacy of the table, but first they had to be fattened on grain. Hence the swan pit. The Great Hospital, in Bishopgate, Norwich, established its swan pit in the Middle Ages, and it still exists. The pit was rebuilt in 1793 by the architect William Ivory and was connected to the nearby river by a pipe. Swans were fattened here until grain shortages brought the practice to a halt. There were records of Great Hospital swans being sent to royal tables, and in one case, to the Pope.

Sedgeford Magazine stands beside the Peddars Way just outside the village. It is thought to have been built by Sir Hamon Le Strange about 1640 as an armoury for muster weapons of the Smithdon Hundred. In 1857 it was bought by Charles Neville-Rolfe, who carved decorations and verses on some of the interior beams. It was also once used as a lodging house for labourers engaged in harvest work. A tiny Victorian militia gunpowder store, in Quebec Road, Dereham, was given to the town in 1987. It dates from about 1860.

Nelson's other column, at South Denes, Yarmouth, was built in 1817 and based on a monument to the Fire of London. It is 20 years older than Nelson's Column in Trafalgar Square and stands 144ft high, topped by Britannia ruling the waves. Oddly, she faces inland, towards Yarmouth's port and Nelson's birthplace, Burnham Thorpe.

Sutton windmill, built in 1789 complete with nine storeys and a cap, is the highest in Norfolk. On a clear day 20 churches are said to be visible from the top. Talking of heights, Westwick's obelisk rises 90ft. It was built by John Petre about 1779 and includes a spiral staircase leading to an octagonal observation chamber. One local tale suggested it had something to do with 18th century rivalry between Westwick and Worstead; but Mr Petre probably just liked the view.

The first concrete bridge in England is thought to be that over the river Waveney at Homersfield. It was built about 1869 by the splendidly-named Sir Shafto Adair, and links Suffolk with Norfolk. It was in a poor state a few years ago and was taken over by the Norfolk and Suffolk Historic Trusts. During the building of Breydon bridge, Yarmouth's second river crossing, the resident engineer had a sign in his office which read: "If you build a bridge you make a friend."

A village hall built of wood and corrugated iron was given to Anmer by King George V and Queen Mary. It had wood panelled walls decorated with photographs of the Royal family, and a coal fire.

Founded in 1951, Wymondham College, for borders and day pupils, is one of the largest schools of its kind in Europe. Some of the buildings, however, are as old as world war two - a set of "temporary" Nissen huts originally built on an old army base which later became a hospital for wounded American airmen. In 1986, the College claimed to have supplied the RAF with more officers than any other school. Nissen huts survive at Bodney army camp, too.

Restoration of the isolated railway halt at County School, near North Elmham - passenger services ceased in 1964 and freight services in 1981 - was being undertaken at the time of writing. The original school, known as Norfolk County School, was opened by the Rev I L Brereton, of Little Massingham, the foundation stone being laid on Easter Monday, 1873, by the Prince of Wales, later King Edward VII. It was an impressive building, but the school lasted only until 1895 and for a time stood empty and remote in its 60-acre grounds. In 1901 the property was taken over by E H Watts as an additional home for Barnado boys, and in 1903 it was ear-marked as a training place for selected Barnado boys destined for careers in the Royal or Merchant Navy. The cost of furnishing the establishment for 300 boys and staff was defrayed by Mr Fenwick Watts, in memory of his father. Watts Naval Training School was opened by Viscount Cole in 1906, complete with dining room, nautical classrooms, hall, chapel and library. The training school was later demolished and the chapel converted into a house. All that really remains from those days is a tiny, poignant and little visited cemetery, set about by trees and now on private land, containing a handful of graves, mainly of boys who died during the years when the school was occupied. The stones show most of them to have been in their early teens.

The origins of Thetford Grammar School lie in a bequest of money and property in a will of 1566. Burston Strike School is a memorial to the longest strike in British history. In 1914, when teachers Tom and Annie Higdon were dismissed from the village county school, the 68 pupils went on strike. For a time they were taught on the village green, then in a workshop. But in 1917 the strike school was opened, funded by trades unions and supporters. Stone tablets on the exterior walls record the donors, including the Sunderland Women's Labour League, the Workers' Suffrage Movement, and the Portmanteau and Trunk Makers' Society of Manchester. Not until 1939 did the Strike School close. It is now a museum.

This is the poignant and isolated little cemetery once attached to the Watts' training complex at County School.

Travellers on the A146 bypass at Gillingham, near Beccles, may catch a glimpse of a frontage of Italian design. It is the Church of Our Lady of Perpetual Succour, the Byzantine-style Roman Catholic church of Gillingham. John Kenyon of Gillingham Hall abandoned Anglicanism in the 1860s, visited Rome, fought to keep the Pope's territory independent, and spent six months in prison. He built the church in 1886, deliberately echoing the Italian style.

Norfolk's oldest surviving council houses are thought to be those at St Mary's Crescent, Thetford, built in 1911. Elsewhere, some were built of clay lump. A row which once stood at Garboldisham, dating to 1917, were said to have been designed by George Skipper, who built Norwich's Royal Arcade.

The word bungalow came from the Hindi word bangla, which meant the home of a European in India. In 1894, Brewer's Dictionary of Phrase & Fable pointed out there were some English bungalows "on the Norfolk coast near Cromer." Somewhat more substantial than the traditional bungalow, Pond Farm at Frans Green, near Dereham, was built during world war two as an American air force headquarters, and is said to be bombproof. Many homes have an adjacent garage. Pond Farm has an adjacent aircraft hangar. There are a number of post world war two prefabricated houses still to be seen. Those at Wymondham's Silfield estate in Park Lane were built in 1948 and given a predicted 15-year life span. Nearly 50 years on they are, by and large, still liked by their residents.

When Norwich's new City Hall was built just before the outbreak of world war two the city gave itself two curious heraldic lions, sculpted by Alfred J Hardiman, which stand on either side of the steps leading to the main doors. Curious, because they sport feminine hair-dos and masculine muscles. Closer inspection, though, suggests they are probably sexless. One story, no doubt apocryphal, says this was not always so and that a saw was produced and certain offending items hastily removed before the official unveiling; and that to this day someone has some unusual souvenirs rolling around in the back of a drawer. Incidentally, the three sculpted figures, also by Hardiman, which overlook City Hall's rear car park, depict Recreation, Wisdom and Education.

In 1970 Miss May Savidge, then aged 77, moved house from Ware, in Hertfordshire, to Wells. Quite literally. The piles of numbered bricks, timbers and windows previously known as Ware Hall House, Ware, were delivered by lorry to the new site at Plummer's Hill, Wells. Whereupon Miss Savidge set to work to rebuild it. Helpers were taken on, but the bulk of the work was done by Miss Savidge, who lived in a caravan until she had a roof over her head.

Hunstanton's Smithdon High School, opened in 1954, was described at the time as a building that "aroused considerable architectural excitment." Over the years students and visitors from all parts of the world have paid respectful visits. It was said to be the building that launched "the New Brutalism." And a visiting American architect once argued there were only two buildings in East Anglia with worldwide reputations - King's College, Cambridge, and Smithdon School.

As the cold blast of the Cold War has warmed, so many of the underground nuclear monitoring posts formally used by the Royal Observer Corps have been closed or sold off. Latest underground item on the market at the time of writing, and the largest, is the Government bunker visible from Norwich southern bypass near Bawburgh. Built in 1955, some 200ft deep and protected by blast-proof walls and cast iron blast doors, it would have housed

150 people in the event of nuclear war. It also stored enough tinned and dehydrated food for 150 people for a month. The bunker - for several decades the media was not supposed to report its location, or its name - was a three-level sector operations centre known as SRHQ41 and would have slotted into the Home Office's network of wartime local government stations.

Seven years ago Norwich council workers engaged in clearing a house after an elderly woman had been admitted to hospital found in a cupboard under the stairs a hoard of pre-war margarine. In all, there were 48 half-pound packs of Echo margarine, still in good condition. Each pack carried the price of two and a half pence per lb. The manufacturers dated the cache to 1937.

Construction of the Castle Mall shopping centre in the heart of Norwich required the excavation of 800,000 tons of soil, enough to fill Trafalgar Square to the height of Nelson's Column. An ornate iron bridge, which first spanned the Wensum in 1882 and which had been in store for 30 years, decorates the entrance to the Mall's No1 car park.

In 1975 a Surrey man named Hippisley, watching a TV programme, suddenly heard his name mentioned. The references also gave an address: Hippisley Hut in Old Hunstanton. Further research indicated that this was where his father, Cmdr R J B Hippisley, was stationed during world war one. Cmdr Hippisley was an early pioneer of wireless telegraphy, and when war broke out he thought he might be able to intercept German signals which directed fleet and Zeppelin movements. Thus Old Hunstanton became the first of a chain of listening posts. Local people nicknamed the wooden building the Hippisley Hut.

Half-a-dozen postal wall-boxes dating from 1861-71 are thought to remain in Norfolk, probably the oldest being an 1861 example at Bramerton. The oldest Victorian pillarbox is said to be that facing the market on The Walk in the city. A Penfold-type box, it dates from between 1866 and 1879. A few years ago over 200 Victorian mail boxes were still in use in the county.

There are 531 parishes in Norfolk, and 464 of them are large enough to have parish councils. Others have parish meetings, the smallest unit in the British democratic system.

Over 920 churches were built in Norfolk between the 11th and 16th centuries - thanks to large populations and great wealth in the Middle Ages - which is more than in any other county. Over 600 are still in use, but there are also more ruined medieval churches in Norfolk than in the rest of the English counties put together. Norfolk also leads the way with its collection of round towered churches, some thought to be Saxon. The county has about 120 of them.

There are a number of candidates for the site of the area's oldest church. Babingley is one. St Felix may have founded the first church in East Anglia on the site of the existing ruined church. There is also a tradition that St Felix built a wooden church at Shernbourne. And the ruined minster at St Elmham, St Cross (Suffolk) may also have been founded by St Felix. Again, a few years ago Suffolk archaeologists working beside the Little Ouse river at Brandon (Suffolk) unearthed a settlement dating from about AD650 which included the remains of a church. Only the timber stains remained, but it had once had three cells, a chancel, nave and annex.

Largest parish church in Norfolk is St Nicholas, Yarmouth. The tallest, at a majestic 160ft, is Cromer. Britain's most easterly church, only a quarter of a mile from the sea, is Christ Church, Lowestoft.

Probably the oldest postal wall-box in Norfolk, this 1861 example is at Bramerton.

As for Norfolk's smallest church, the subject provoked an almighty debate in the EDP a few years ago. Among the candidates were Frenze, Bittering, Swannington, West Caister, Houghton (near South Pickenham), Fishley, and a corrugated iron and timber construction built by Boulton & Paul near the gates of Beeston Hall at Beeston St Andrew. At the time, however, the 30-seat building was listed as a mission church and thus ruled out of the competition. So it was decided that Frenze, within the boundaries of Frenze Hall Farm and standing beside the Angles Way footpath, took the title. More recently, however, an even stronger candidate has emerged: Santon (not Santon Downham). Santon All Saints was built just outside the village in 1628 by Thomas Bancroft who, it is said, was the sole parishioner. Measuring 17ft across the nave and 10ft across the chancel, and with room for only two at a time at the altar rail, it had no lighting or heating.

One of the youngest cathedrals in the country is the Norwich Roman Catholic Cathedral of St John the Baptish in Earlham Road. It was built in the 1880s but was not elevated to cathedral status until 100 years later. In 1963, when the 56lb weathercock was removed from Norwich's Anglican cathedral for repairs, the date 1668 was exposed. In 1986, a Press conference about cathedral repair work was held on a scaffolding platform level with the weathercock, 313ft above the city. The last 160ft to the top had to be climbed on ladders on the outside of the spire. Representatives of the EDP bravely attended. News editors can be cruel, sometimes.

Walsingham Methodist church, founded in 1793, is one of the oldest in East Anglia. John Wesley is thought to have preached there before the church was built. The Free Presbyterian church in Oulton Broad (Suffolk) became affiliated to the Ulster church of the Unionist MP the Rev Ian Paisley in 1985, one of only two such churches in England.

A plaque in St Peter Mancroft, Norwich, says the 5040-change Grandshire Bob Triple was rung there for the first time on May 2, 1715. It took eight ringers over three hours. Wicklewood churchyard entrance includes a small turnstile, a remnant of the days when a National School stood just the other side of the wall. The school was demolished in 1895.

There are thought to be only two church barrel organs in the county, one at Mattishall Burgh and the other at Wood Rising. Each has three barrels of 10 tunes, ranging from the well-known to the totally obscure. Wood Rising's barrel organ was made in 1826.

Wymondham's Roman Catholic church, paid for by subscription, was built in 1952 to commemorate those who died in Japanese prison camps during world war two. The names of about 25,000 British and Allied dead were inscribed in three books by Fr Cowin and, in the main, by Frank Hardy, who took three years over the task.

The remote St Benet's Abbey near Horning, which comes under the Bishopric of Norwich, has a 20ft oak cross erected on the site of the altar. The oak was donated by the Queen, and came from Sandringham.

Norfolk's only parish without a church is Great Palgrave. Three churches - Reepham, Whitwell and Hackford - share a single churchyard at Reepham. Aslacton St Michael may have the oldest peal of five bells in the county - 1604, 1607, 1607, 1607 and 1614 - and all by a single bellfounder.

Walpole St Peter church, and St Peter Mancroft in Norwich, has a foot-path-cum-passage which runs under the sanctuary. West Walton has a detached tower standing on four arches and built on the firmest ground. In 1993, it was calculated that 107 Norfolk churches were home to colonies of bats.

Bowthorpe Worship Centre was unique in East Anglia when it opened in 1986 in that it was the first building to be shared jointly by Anglican, Baptish, Methodist, Roman Catholic, Quaker and United Reformed Church demoninations. It was built next door to the remains of an excavated Saxo-Norman church. One establishment which was lost and is now found is St Nicholas chapel, Itteringham. Although its existence had been known for many years it was not until 1986 that it was spotted as a cropmark on an aerial photograph.

Canon Walter Marcon, rector of St Peter and St Paul at Edgefield for 63 years, was born at the Rectory in 1850 and died in the same room in 1937. On becoming rector, he decided the church was in an isolated position, so he had it dismantled and reassembled half a mile away and closer to the community. The job took two years, from 1883-85.

When a house on Felthorpe Road, Attlebridge, was built in the 1930s it incorporated a miniature church complete with pulpit and pews. Nearby, the builder also constructed a small chapel.

Trinity Hospital almshouses, Castle Rising, were built by Henry Howard, the Earl of Northampton, in 1609, for women of "honest life and conversation, religious, grave, discreet, able to read . . . and no common beggar, harlot, scold, drunkard, haunter of taverns, inns and alehouses."

Several clergymen have gained places in local legend. There was the over excited parson who bowled King Edward V11 for a duck after the King had been persuaded to play in a charity cricket match; the canon, an enthusiastic angler, who was said to have kept minnows in the font; and the vicar of Garboldisham who, in the 1920s, responded to complaints that the parish magazine contained little that was controversial by publishing the village cricket team's batting and bowling averages.

In 1977, Breckland District Council received a planning application for a wayside shrine at Spreadoak Wood, a thin belt of woodland in Bittering Belt, near Longham, close to the site of a 16th century pilgrim resting place. Permission was granted, the plans being "in conformity with the building regulations and the public health acts." The application had been made by Paul Hodac, a Coventry car worker, born 1918, who spent much of his early life in Czechoslovakian Monrovia. In 1939, Hodac and other Czech soldiers slipped into Polish Silesia past German border guards and dogs. He joined the doomed Czech Legion, walked across Poland and into Rumania. Months later he arrived in Marseilles where he joined the Czech army in France, and later fought in Normandy. In 1940 he arrived in England, became a parachute instructor, married and settled. Some 20 years later he spotted an advertisement offering 10 acres of woodland for sale in Norfolk, and he bought it. He started to spend his holidays there, camping in a caravan among the trees, and in 1977 began to build the 16ft by 10ft brick and pantile shrine in the wood on top of a short stretch of surviving Roman road. Five years later Porta Maria was finished, complete with ornamental gates.

In 1984 a Norfolk holidaymaker in Germany reported seeing a double-deck bus with "Loddon" on the route indicator heading down an autobahn. Subsequent investigation showed that the driver was not lost. He was heading for Darmstadt, where ex-Eastern Counties Omnibus, registration number 72 DPW, was to be installed in a bierhall. I heard later the bierhall bartender stood inside the bus and served drinks through a side window. It still sported its Loddon sign and 007 route number.

Adventuring individuals and pioneering groups from the region have been braving the unknown in "foreign parts" for centuries, and there are particularly close historical ties with the eastern seaboard of North America. In the mid-19th century, for example, boats left King's Lynn and Yarmouth every week during the sailing season, mostly bound for Quebec, carrying mainly labouring class emigrants desperate to escape worsening social conditions at home.

Today, familiar place-names are scattered across the maps. There is a Horsham, Anglia, Brandon, Cromer and a Gunton in Canada. In America, there is a Cambridge in Vermont (another in Massachusetts), with a Swanton, Brandon, and a Thetford Hill Forest. In Massachusetts there is a Framlingham, Wells (another in Vermont), Attleborough, Rockland and a Hingham. There is a port of Lynn, and a Yarmouth, which is also represented in Cape Cod. And according to an unofficial count there are also seven Norwichs (Connecticut, Kansas, New York State, two, Vermont, two, Long Island) and six Norfolks (Virginia, two, Maryland, Massachusetts, Nebraska, New York State) in the States, plus another Norwich in Ontario, Canada. In 1986, when a civic party from Yarmouth visited an international gathering in America to mark the 225th anniversary of the founding of Yarmouth, Nova Scotia, they were joined by representatives of the towns of Yarmouth in Maine and Yarmouth, Massachusetts. Of course, my list of regional names duplicated in the New World is by no means complete.

Between 1633 and 1638 about 200 inhabitants of Hingham sailed to the New World, the result being the foundation of Hingham, Mass. One who went in 1637 was Samuel Lincoln, destined to become the first American ancestor of Abraham Lincoln, 16th President of the United States. A bust of Abraham Lincoln in Hingham church commemorates the link.

Over the years some of the ties have been subject to neat historical twists. During world war two some American airmen serving in East Anglia with the 8th Air Force found they had been posted to a base close to the town or village their forebears had left years before.

West Point, New York State, boasts a solid link with Hethel and Bracon Ash - the Townshend Chain. This particular link was forged by a branch of the family which held land in Norfolk in the 16th century. It was the Quaker head of the American branch who, bitterly opposed to British policy during the War of Independence, caused a great chain to be made and stretched across the Hudson river when he heard the British were about to bombard West Point. A surviving section of the chain was later placed on the parade ground at West Point.

A thatched gazebo in the Elizabethan Gardens on Roanoak Island, North Carolina, stands as a memorial to English colonists who went to America. The roof is made of Norfolk reed.

Thomas Paine, the Thetford-born thinker, writer and radical, and another who opposed the aims of the British in America, was the first person to coin the phrase "The United States of America." His statue in Thetford shows him holding a quill and a book, which is wrong way up. This is said to be because his writings turned the world upside down.

Wymondham has a number of connections with North America. It was a Wymondham man, Richard Bucke, who married John Rolfe and the Indian princess Pocahontas in Jamestown, Virginia (see Figures in the Landscape). The descendant of another, Samuel Huntington, signed the Declaration of Independence on behalf of the State of Connecticut, and is said to have founded the towns of Windham and Norwich in that state. Another possible link, with Nantucket Island, is through Peter Foulger, who sailed for New England in 1635 and who subsequently married a Norwich girl. Peter was important to the first settlement of whites on Nantucket in a number of ways, but largely because he could speak to the natives in their own tongue. There is a Peter Foulger Museum in Broad Street, Nantucket.

George Vancouver, born in King's Lynn, who subsequently gave his name to Vancouver, originally claimed Alaska for the Crown under the name of "New Norfolk." Local names brought into use included included Lynn, Holkham Bay, Point Houghton, Point Snettisham, and Point Anmer.

Norwich's replica of the Liberty Bell, from Norwich, Connecticut, was presented in 1893 by Emma Lathrop of Newark, New Jersey, a descendant of Christopher Huntingdon, who on November 1, 1660, became the first-born male child in Norwich, Connecticut.

Captain John Mason, also born in Lynn, in 1586, was an adventurer, colonial governor, merchant, army paymaster, visionary and pirate. He left an American estate of 2000 acres to the town of Lynn for a rent of one penny a year, but he also decreed in his will that Lynn should send five families to New Hampshire to settle it. The corporation, fighting shy of the cost of shipping the families abroad, dithered endlessly, and in 1654 finally gave the estate to Robert Greene of Swaffham. Mason, who founded the state of New Hampshire, died in 1635 and was buried in Westminster Abbey. The piracy occurred in his early days when he leased the Scottish island of Rona and used it as a base from which to raid ships plying between Scotland and Norway.

In the 1890s Richard Laxen and Sid Thirkettle, from Aylsham, emigrated to Canada. For a time they worked for Canadian Pacific Railway, but in 1914 settled in Saskatchewan and became farmers. Other settlers duly arrived, and the Norfolk men named the new community Aylsham, after their native village. In 1938, Richard Laxen, who served with the Canadian forces in Europe during world war one, brought his family back to England. They settled at Holt and Richard died in 1954. In the late 1970s contact between the two Aylshams was established again and there were exchanges of visitors and gifts.

One of the prisoners transported with the First Fleet to Australia in 1788 was Henry Cabell, of Norwich, who married fellow prisoner Susannah Holmes while in Norwich prison. Cabell is now an Australian folk hero, for he is thought to have been the first white man ashore in what is now New South Wales. He was carrying the ship's captain at the time. Henry and Susannah eventually built up a profitable mercantile business and also found time to have 10 children. Henry's likeness can be seen in the dungeons at Norwich Castle Museum. Incidentally, I once came across an unsubstantiated reference which suggested that the first true white child born on Australian soil was delivered at Sydney Cove in 1788 of a mother, presumably a prisoner, said to have come from Hethersett.

Thetford's statue of Thomas Paine, who is holding the Rights of Man upside down.

An English oak seat on Lord Howe Island, overlooking Blackburn Island, New South Wales, was built and paid for by public subscription in Norfolk. Guiding hand behind the project was the late Derek Neville, writer, poet and restaurateur, then of Itteringham, who researched the life of David Blackburn, a Norwich man who sailed as an officer with the First Fleet. Neville discovered that a tiny island off Lord Howe Island was named after Blackburn in 1788, though modern maps marked it as Rabbit Island. Thanks to Neville's campaigning it is now known as Blackburn Island once again. Over 2000 Norfolk people subscribed to the cost of the seat and its transportation to Australia.

In 1988, the Lord Mayor of Hobart, Australia, Mrs Doone Kennedy, visited Blickling Hall at the invitation of the then Lord Mayor of Norwich, David Bradford. The city of Hobart was founded by the Hobart family, who built Blickling. Mrs Kennedy's mother originated from Itteringham, a few miles from Blickling.

Former Lyng couple Jim and Dorothy Curzon decided in 1987 to organise a barbecue for Norfolk exiles at Currumbin, on the Queensland coast. In nine weeks they made contact with 156 eligible families, mainly within 100 miles of Brisbane. Indeed, so many turned up for the barbecue they decided to form a Norfolk and Norwich Association. The last I heard over 500 families were registered members.

The East Anglian Society of New Zealand has been active for 20 years. What is more, it has introduced Iceni Day to that part of the world, when members gather for picnics, mardles (meaning jaw-jaw), and even dwile flonking (see Simple Diversions), which may have taken longer to explain to the natives.

One New Zealand construction firm with Norfolk connections once produced ranges of homes including the Breydon and the Brundall. And the oldest wooden house in New Zealand, at Kerikeri, is thought to have been built in about 1820 by James Kemp, a Wymondham blacksmith who became a missionary.

There is a connection between Kimberley, near Wymondham, and Kimberley in South Africa, which was named after Sir John Wodehouse, first Earl of Kimberley, who died in 1902. Kimberley, in Cape Province, was founded in 1870 on the discovery of diamonds. Kimberlite, incidentally, meaning igneous rock consisting largely of periodite and often containing diamonds, is a 19th century word also derived from Kimberley. Sir Benjamin D'Urban, of Shotesham All Saints, is said to have given his name to Durban. Planned and laid out by the Dutch in 1834, it was occupied by British troops under D'Urban in 1842.

Links between Norfolk and Norfolk Island, a dot in the Pacific 930 miles north-east of Sydney, were strengthened in 1980 with the arrival in Norwich of a flag sent by the president of the legislative assembly of Norfolk Island to Norfolk County Council. Earlier, the council had sent a message of congratulation and a tankard to the island's newly-formed assembly. The island was discovered by Captain Cook in 1774 and named after the family of the Duke of Norfolk.

Lord Buxton and his daughter Cindy celebrated a unique double in 1988 when it was announced that a glacier on remote South Georgia Island was to be named after the family in recognition of film-maker Cindy's month there in 1982 when she and Annie Price were stranded at the outset of the Falklands' War. Buxton Glacier is in St Andrew's Bay. Talking of the Falklands, in 1984 a soldier with Norfolk connections erected a sign on a Port Stanley telegraph pole which read: "Poringland, 8200 miles."

In the 1840s a Blo Norton labourer headed for the South Seas, became a successful sugar planter, and married into the island's royal family. He was Lord Charles Notley, a member of the Upper House of Parliament of the Sandwich Islands - an early name for the Hawaiian Islands. In 1882 he revisited Blo Norton and paid for the church porch to be rebuilt, and in 1886 returned a second time to adopt his neice Emma and to provide the church with a sixth bell.

Burnham Thorpe's Sicilian connection began in 1799 after Nelson's victory in the Battle of the Nile. Nelson was made Duke of Bronte, a town on the slopes of Mount Etna. In 1985 a twinning ceremony between Bronte and Burnham Thorpe took place. Samples of Nelson's Blood (spiced rum) were taken to Sicily.

In 1987 a picture of an officer of the East Norfolk (9th Foot) Regiment, in 18th century uniform, appeared on a postage stamp issued by the Caribbean island of St Kitts. The East Norfolk was one of the regiments which originally fought the French for possession of the island.

4: Figures in the Landscape

Sandringham estate was purchased by Edward, Prince of Wales, in 1861, though I once heard a whisper that Buckenham Tofts, a sport ing estate now demolished and incorporated in the Stanford Battle Area, was one of the other possibilities at the time. The selection of Buckenham Tofts, particularly, in preference to Sandringham, would have had a profound effect on modern maps of Norfolk. No railway line from Lynn to New Hunstanton. No New Hunstanton come to that. And certainly no Stanford Battle Area.

Informality and relaxation are the Sandringham keynotes today. Privately, the Queen rides through woods and across farmland, in raincoat and headscarf, or walks accompanied by dogs. She joins shooting parties, drives on public roads, and has been known to pop into local shops. The Queen and Queen Mother are members of the local Women's Institute, listening to the entertainment and the speakers, pouring tea for their table companions. In fact, the Queen Mother hardly missed a January meeting of the Sandringham branch since her first attendance, with Queen Mary, in 1937. The Queen and Queen Mother both attended the branch's 70th anniversary meeting at West Newton village hall in 1989. Incidentally, Norfolk Constabulary is entrusted with the security of the Royal family at Sandringham. Elsewhere, security is the responsibility of the Metropolitan Police. The Norfolk tradition is said to be by previous Royal request. And the Norwich Gates, the great ornamental wrought iron gates at the entrance to Sandringham House, were presented by the people of Norfolk to Edward, Prince of Wales, as a wedding present.

To qualify for the award of a Royal warrent, goods or services have to be supplied to the relevant Royal household for at least three years. Warrent holders have their own association and they often gather at the annual Sandringham flower show. There are about 50 local traders on the list, including a Lynn fish merchant, a Dersingham newsagent, a Brandon field gate maker, a Sedgeford builder, an Ingoldisthorpe carpet firm, a Norwich Christmas cracker factory and a Hillington supplier of farm lime.

A few years ago the vicar of Binham Priory, leafing through the visitors' book for 1986, came across the names of the Queen, the Queen Mother and Prince Charles. The Queen Mother's name appeared at the end of October and the Queen's and Prince Charles' names the following January. A case of Royal recommendation, perhaps.

A lovesick swain once popped the question by advertising on the electronic scoreboard at Norwich City's Carrow Road football ground. "Sandra, will you marry me when the time is right? I love you so much." Egged on by an enthusiastic 18,000 crowd, Sandra was reported to have said, "Yes."

In 1987 a Horsham St Faith woman married her step brother, whose father was married to her mother. The ceremony ended with the bride receiving a hug from her step-father who had just become her father-in-law.

A baby born at the Norfolk and Norwich Hospital in 1986 weighed in at 12lb 5oz. But it was not a record. Sixteen years earlier, at the same hospital, a baby boy clipped the scales at 12lb 6oz. Then again, in 1927 a Walpole St Andrew lady evidently gave birth to a son weighing 13lb 12oz.

Roadside trader Peter Hawes welded himself inside his layby cafe in 1993 in a battle for compensation from the Department of Transport after the DoT closed the layby on safety grounds. Fed by well-wishers and family, he stayed inside for six months. And in August, 1989, Andrew Pearson of Longham finally achieved his ambition of sleeping in the garden under canvas for 10 years. At the age of nine he decided to sleep under canvas for a decade, to set a new record, a bid which was threatened only once, in 1987, when the tent collapsed on top of him during a storm.

Telephone directories can sometimes reveal some fascinating surnames. Finds glimpsed in the Norwich phonebook over the years have included St George at Reepham, Guy Fawkes at Fakenham, Jesus at Acle and Gotobed at Great Snoring.

Talking of names, the eye department at Norwich's West Norwich Hospital is called the Nelson ward!

John Parker of Wingfield (Suffolk) is famous for driving the Norwich Union coach and team of greys. He once beat the world coach driving endurance record, set in 1888, with a 136-mile run from London to Bristol in 17hr 15min. In 1986 he completed a 257-mile run from Norwich to Antwerp, and he and his grooms changed a team of four horses in 27.69sec to beat the previous world record.

Nick Crane, of Cringleford, and cousin Richard, having cycled up Mount Kilimanjaro and jogged the length of the Himalayas to raise funds for Intermediate Technology, in 1986 cycled 3294 miles to reach the world's most remote spot. The journey took them from Bangladesh to the Dzungarian desert, near China's north border. They reported it "hot, horrible and singularly uninspiring."

In 1993, nine-year-old diabetic Joseph (Little Joe) Lambert, of Beccles, became the youngest person to walk the 875 miles from Land's End to John O' Groats. He completed the journey in 40 days raising money for research into diabetes. Prior to this exploit he had already climbed more than 200 mountains and completed eight long distant walks.

The Norfolk Gates at Sandringham - a wedding present from the county.

A year or so ago two four- and five-year-old boys joined the reception class at Brundall primary school. Although unrelated, and although they had never even met before, they were both named Matthew David Tremayne.

Sheikh Hamdan Al Maktoum, from Dubai, reputedly the richest racehorse owner and breeder in the world, bought the 5000-acre Shadwell estate, near Brettenham, in 1984. The Melton and Snare Hill studs were already well established, but two years later one of the most lavish studs in Europe, the Nunnery, also opened its doors.

In 1993, Vincent Thurkettle, of Great Hockham, became Britain's champion gold panner when he won the national prospecting finals at Wanlockhead in Dumfries and Galloway. He beat nearly 50 other competitors and took the title after taking 5min 21sec to find 14 tiny flakes of gold hidden in 40lb of sand and gravel.

Surgeon Ken McKee began to work on the development of artificial joint replacements several decades ago, but it was not until 1951 that the first total hip replacement operation was developed and completed at the Norfolk and Norwich Hospital. At the hospital, surgeons have since developed the "Norwich hip," which is said to be more durable than other types.

In 1986, Lord Addington of Thorpe Hamlet became the youngest peer in the Upper House. He was then 23. Dominic Bryce Hubbard, the 6th Baron Addington, was the latest in the line which began in 1887. Born in Suffolk, Lord Addington attended the Hewett School, Norwich, and City College, Norwich.

Wells couple Frank and Margaret Dye were selected by an American sailing magazine to its Hall of Fame. They had crossed the North Sea to Norway and Iceland, sailed 2000 miles along the coast of America, and cruised around the Persian Gulf. All in a 15ft Wayfarer. Still at Wells, in 1987 Bishop Ingle House celebrated 25 years of providing low cost holidays for clergy and their families. The home was established by George Ingle, of Wells, who became Bishop of Fulham and Willesden.

One man has a railway signal named after him. Les King of Wymondham, who once drove diesel shunter engines, has his name on a plaque on a restored signal which once stood at the Browick crossing and is now kept at Wymondham station.

Brickyard Close, Costessey, had lots of neighbourliness, and in 1986 the residents celebrated 60 years of living close together. Of the 13 homes, 10 were then owned by members of the Barnes family, and the rest by family friends. It all began in 1926 when James Barnes bought two acres of land and moved his family there. A brickyard worker, he began to build his own home. So Barnes folk dug the wells, made the bricks, and built the houses.

Scattered families like to get together, too, and some hold special gatherings. These include - FAIRHEAD: centered on Bedingham (Suffolk) church, near Bungay; FILBY: they meet at Filby village, members travelling from Australia and America; KIDNER: over 100 from Britain and abroad gathered at Poringland in 1988; MASSINGHAM: they return to local roots at Langham; THIRST: first reunion at Thirst's Farm, East Ruston, in 1979, many of their grandparents having been born at the farm in the 1800s; and ULPH: they gathered at Burnham Market.

The last 25 years has seen a huge increase in interest in tracing roots. The EDP, particularly in the 1970s and 1980s, received many inquiries and visitors, mainly from America, Canada, Australia, New Zealand and occasionally South Africa. In 1987 an American millionaire from Virginia, tracing his family tree in Norfolk, bought freehold premises in St Giles, Norwich, for the Norwich and District Genealogical Society. It is the only one in Britain to have its own property.

Abroad, hundreds of people can sometimes trace their roots to a single person. There are over 100 HOWLETT families in Adelaide, nearly all of them descended from William Howlett, who was 16 when he reached South Australia in the ship Emma in 1836. HAZELL is another well documented Australian name. They derive from William Hazell, of Norfolk, who was 28 when convicted of sheep stealing and sentenced to transportation. He arrived on the prison ship HMS Chas Kerr in 1837, and eventually became a policeman. The TUFTS took another direction. Peter Tufts of Wilby, Eccles Road, sailed for America in 1636. His brick garrison house was said to be one of the oldest in America, and one of his descendants founded Tufts University. In about 1840, four more Tufts from Scoulton Mere settled in Canada and named their village Tuftsville, now Madoc Junction, Ontario. Another descendant, Sonny Tufts, was a movie star during world war two. In 1985 the Tufts Kinsmen, with members in America and Canada, made a first pilgrimage back to Norfolk.

At Caister, you are likely to hear more nicknames than usual. Most relate to fishing families, which often used them to differentiate between people of the same name. Thus Wampoo, Teapot West and Crip Green. Skipper Woodhouse's nickname came from his headgear. His brother David was Crewger, while sister Rosie was known as Kitten. Of the Brown family, father Emmanuel was Mab, his son became Maybee and his grandson Young Maybee. Then there was Lightning Brown, Puddings Brown and Solly Brown. There was also a Shell George and Rouse George, Sweeping, and Geesh (who once did a concert piece based on geisha girls). A few years ago the Caister lifeboat crew included Flowerpot Man (a horticulturalist), Snuffy, Benny, and Reuters (the local newspaper correspondent).

In 1986, a Bristol motorist who set out to drive to Yarmouth gave up eight hours later. He (or she) evidently stopped on the M4 to ask the way - having already been to Birmingham - only to be told she (or he) was exactly seven miles from home near Bristol. Or 300 miles off course. And in 1993 a Norfolk motorist began a drive from Middlesbrough to Norwich. She set off at 11.45pm on Tuesday; was lost near Durham at 2.35am on Wednesday; reached Edinburgh at 6am; was escorted south by the police and ran out of petrol at Wetherby at 10am (40 miles from her starting point); and at 6pm was escorted from Wetherby to Norwich by her mother, reaching home 18 hours after leaving Middlesbrough. She had driven well over 1000 miles and spent £80 on petrol.

The Singing Postman, Allan Smethurst, once made a Norfolk dialect song more popular than the Beatles. His ditty, "Hev you got a loight, boy," became a chart success in 1965 and for a while even outsold the Fab Four.

One of the smallest homes in the county was that of retired circus clown Marcus le Touche. At one time he lived beside the river at Burgh next Aylsham in the cab of a homemade boat-shaped caravan trailer, the cab floor measuring roughly 6ft 9in by 3ft 6in. Marcus, alias Clown Roma, of Hugenot descent, retired in 1986 at the age of 78 and donated his costume to Norwich Stranger's Hall Museum.

Jenny Lind, known as the Swedish Nightingale because of her voice, founded the children's hospital in Norwich which still carries her name. Two city concerts in 1849 raised the money, and the Jenny Lind Infirmary for Sick Children (now the children's unit at the Norwich and Norwich Hospital) opened in 1853.

The late Marcus le Touche, alias Clown Roma, pictured beside the river at Burgh next Aylsham with his dog Viscount.

The Rev Bartholomew Edwards (1789-1889) was rector of Ashill for 76 years, while Jack Spark was clerk to Horsford parish council for 50 years. Appointed in 1937, he missed only two meetings through illness. Hugh "Sonny" Harwood was Yarmouth's longest serving beach boy. He joined his father in 1926 in selling buns on the beach and for over 40 years tended beach huts and hired out deck chairs. He could recall days when 700 deckchairs were hired out at 2d a time and four pleasure boats plied from the beach to Scroby sands.

In 1986, on the eve of her 105th birthday, Ada Fakes become the oldest known person to fly in a helicopter. The flight took her over Winterton, where she was born.

Inventor of the modern toilet is said to have been Sir John Harington, godson of Queen Elizabeth 1, who designed a flushing water closet. He built one at his home in 1596 and persuaded the Queen to have one installed at Richmond. Unfortunately, he subsequently wrote a book about it titled "The Metamorphosis of Ajax" (evidently a pun on the word jakes, an old expression for a privvy). The Queen was not amused, and Harington left the court. The ballcock was invented in 1748, enabling Joseph Bramah to patent his improved flush toilet in 1778 and inspiring Thomas Crapper, who is thought to have been involved in work at Sandringham House, to continue its development into the next century. Joshua Jeremiah Phillpot was another major figure in the toilets scene.

But did Harington develop the first flushing loo? Prior to the building of Norwich's new magistrates' courts in Palace Plain, archaeologists unearthed the remains of a 12th century Norman house complete with the country's earliest known self-flusher. It evidently drew its motive power from the rise and fall of tides on the nearby river Wensum.

Manor Farm at Bale once boasted a four-hole outside toilet - three adult and one child, with two "waiting" seats. The most swanky urinal in the county was probably that at Wolferton railway station, where guests for Sandringham arrived and departed by train. The urinal was built next to the waiting room in 1898 by the then Prince of Wales. It is thought the Tsar of Russia used the facilities. King Alfonso probably did. And Edward V11 certainly did.

Doughty's Hospital, Norwich, celebrated its 300th anniversary in 1987 and dates from the building of almshouses in 1687 with money bequeathed by William Doughty of Dereham. The origins of Pulham St Mary Pennoyers VC primary school also went back over 300 years when villagers active in the Guild of St James built a chapel where Walter Colman, the hermit of Pulham, could offer daily prayer. A 1674 will of William Pennoyers noted that two widows were paid for teaching there, and directed that the proceeds of the manor should go towards paying them.

Old documents reveal some marvellous names. In 1715 there was an Ague at Geldeston, a Fishhook at Holme next Sea and at Yarmouth, a Heron at Hickling and a Worm at Holt. In 1705, Beeston next Mileham boasted a Longstraw, Terrington St Clement had a Dornaile, and Lynn the delightfully named Marmaduke Bootflower. In the diaries of the Rev Benjamin Armstrong, vicar of Dereham (1850-88) there is an entry for December 25, 1867, which reads: "Married young parishioner of the name of Mahershallalashbaz Tuck. His father wanted to call him by the shortest name in the Bible, and for the purpose selected Uz. But, the clergyman making some demur, the father said in pique, 'Well, if he cannot have the shortest he shall have the longest.'"

Professor Dorothy Hodgkin was awarded the Nobel Prize for chemistry in 1964, and in 1977 was elected president of the British Association for the Advancement of Science, only the second woman to have held the post at that time. Early in her life she lived at Beccles and Geldeston, attended the Sir John Leman School in Beccles, and was awarded Freedom of the town in 1965.

In 1953, Sir Edmund Hillary, fresh from his successful ascent of Everest, and being hotly pursued by the media, went into hiding at the home of a friend of his sister, who lived in Norwich. Sir Edmund apparently stayed for a couple of days, catching his breath before another round of crowds and interviews.

Experiments with hovercraft began in the early 1950s conducted by Sir Christopher Cockerell, who then lived at Blundeston. He worked out the principles of using air to reduce friction using a hairblower, a length of tubing and a couple of tins. Later, the first working model of a hovercraft was built at an Oulton Broad (Suffolk) boatyard - using a model aeroplane engine - and tested at Somerleyton Hall on the Waveney. The first commercial version crossed the Channel on July 5, 1959.

During world war two, and immediately after Dunkirk, Norwich, traditionally a hotbed of radicalism, was reported to have the highest ratio of concientious objectors per population in the country.

Every year for several years in the 1980s a lady booked into a Norwich hotel, watched the city's Battle of Britain flypast and parade, and later visited Blickling Hall. The Hall, now in the care of the National Trust, was one of the last war's more ornate billets for RAF personnel stationed at the nearby Oulton air base. And this is the clue. The lady, known simply as "D," or "Doreen," regularly penned verses after her visit which she invariably sent to Blickling. The verses suggested that "Doreen" was the girlfriend of a flier who presumably lost his life on active service. She always remained anonymous.

Former MP and Freeman of London, Sir William Steward, is thought to have been largely responsible for introducing the British to curry. Educated at the Norwich Model School, he bought one of Britain's first curry restaurants in 1933. In 1962 he founded Veraswamy's Food Products, and put curry in cans and on general sale in the High Street. He also created many curry powders, sauces, chutneys and pickles.

Incidentally, several current Freemen of London live in Norfolk. Among other things, they are entitled to drive sheep through the streets of London and to be hung with a silken rope.

Lord High Admiral of the Wash is the title which gave the Le Strange family of Hunstanton the right to the North-West Norfolk foreshore. Folklore had it than in 1929, when long distance swimmer and glamour girl Mercedes Gleitz became the first person to swim the Wash, she was met on Hunstanton beach by the Squire who said: "You do understand, madam, that everything washed up on this beach belongs to me."

Dr Sydney Long (1870-1939), born in Wells, founded Norfolk Naturalists' Trust in 1926, the first county conservation trust in Britain. He bought the 400-acre Cley Marshes, and a week later, hosting a dinner at the George Hotel, Cley, proposed the formation of a trust to acquire and manage nature reserves of its own. Incidentally, the Norfolk and Norwich Naturalists' Society, founded in 1869, was also the first society of its kind in the country.

Edith Cavell, executed by the Germans during world war one, is honoured in Newfoundland, and I believe a Nursing Sunday was held annually in St John's. An Edith Cavell Lodge was founded there in the 1920s by the Loyal Orange Benevolent Society, there was a Cavell Avenue in St John's, and girls were given the name Cavell as a Christian name. There is an even loftier memorial to the lady - the 11,000ft Mount Cavell in the Canadian Rockies. In Jasper Park, it overlooks a Cavell memorial chapel beside the Lake of Forgiveness.

The exploits of Ada Cole, of Croxton, near Thetford, have tended to become overshadowed by memories of Edith. Ada, born 1860, became a district nurse and made her home at Cley. Travelling to Belgium to see her sister, who was a nun, she was so appalled at the way horses were treated she began a campaign which led to the formation of the International League for the Protection of Horses. She worked as a Red Cross nurse near Antwerp and was eventually arrested by the Germans for helping Allied troops to escape across the border. Miss Cole was also sentenced to death by firing squad, but escaped the fate of Edith Cavell because the war ended before sentence could be carried out.

To Swaffham-born man Howard Carter, a gifted artist with a fascination for Egyptology, went the honour of discovering the tomb of Tutankhamun in 1922, thus winning worldwide acclaim while working under the sponsorship of Lord Carnarvon. Carter died in 1939 and was buried at Putney Vale cemetery, London.

There is a local connection with that all-purpose expletive, "Gordon Bennett!" James Gordon Bennett (1795-1872) was founder and editor of the New York Herald, and in 1906 a memorial Gordon Bennett hot air balloon race was held from Paris. The second placed balloon, piloted by the Hon Charles Rolls, landed at Sandringham, while the third placed balloon (Henri de la Vauls) evidently came down at Walsingham.

Overstrand used to be the "village of millionaires." Caught in the Poppyland boom of the late 1880s, the pace of change quickened further when Lord Battersea moved there. The architect Edward Lutyens was brought in, and big houses and important and titled people followed. Royalty were among the visitors. So were Sir Beerbohm and Lady Tree, Sir Henry Irvine and Winston Churchill, while W G Grace and Ranjitsinghi flexed their muscles on the local cricket pitch. By the end of world war one, however, Overstrand was no longer fashionable and the trippers preferred Yarmouth.

A bicycle on Fakenham's town sign commemorates John Garrood, born 1852. A bicycle manufacturer in the 1870s, he was the first to build bikes using tubes for the forks. Alas, his patents were infringed. The sign also has an ox-wagon, which recalls Henry Buckenham, born 1844, a Methodist missionary. He established a mission on the Orange River and in 1889, accompanied by his wife and two others, trekked from Kimberley to the Zambesi, a distance of 2000 miles, in four years and eight months. Henry died in 1896 and was buried on the banks of the Zambesi.

Another local man closely connected with the development of Africa was the Rev John Colense, who became rector of Forncett St Mary in 1845, established a school in Forncett St Peter, and who was offered the bishopric of Natal in 1853. Colense, with his family and a band of parishioners, founded a settlement called New Forncett in the South African veldt, but he came into conflict with the primate of Capetown. Colense was subsequently charged with heresy but won his case before the Privy Council in 1866 and ultimately befriended the Zulu king Cetewayo. Colense continued to preach peace as the impi legions and British troops went to war, but the effort and strain took its toll. He died in 1883.

The family name of Gurney has been linked with banking and Quakerism for many years, but Gurneys have lived in Norfolk since the Conquest. In 1770 John and Henry Gurney set up a bank in Norwich which became Gurney & Co, and in 1807 Samuel Gurney - with the Norwich bank in the care of Joseph John and Daniel - went to London and became a partner in a firm which became Overend, Gurney & Co. His sons carried on the business until 1865 when it was made into a joint stock company. In 1866, at the height of railway mania, the bank failed with liabilities of over £71 million. Many investors and firms went under. The Norwich bank, however, flourished, and was absorbed by Barclays in 1896. Joseph John Gurney (1788-1847), in addition to his banking interests, was also a minister of the Society of Friends and an advocate of prison reform and the abolition of slavery.

Bowler hats, known in America as the Derby, were popularised by Norfolk landowner William Coke in about 1850. Because he found his tall riding hat frequently swept off by overhanging branches, he asked his hatters to design a lower-crowned hat. The first was made from felt supplied by Thomas and William Bowler.

The first operation under anaesthetic in Norfolk is believed to have been carried out at the Norfolk and Norwich Hospital in January, 1847. A young woman inhaled the "ethereal fumes" and had a leg amputated. She was insensible to the pain and sang psalms throughout, apparently.

Imposing grave of Robert Hales, the Norfolk Giant, at West Somerton.

Robert Hales, the Norfolk giant, is buried at West Somerton. Born in 1820, he reached 7ft 8in and 33st. As a young man Hales went to sea, but later he began touring England, at first with his sister Mary (7ft 2in), who died aged 20. Hales met Royalty, including Queen Victoria, who gave him a gold watch and chain, and he also toured America. Later in life he kept a pub in Sheffield, and died in 1863 on a visit to Yarmouth.

In 1811 ex-convict John Thurston wrote to Norfolk from Botany Bay and reported, among other things, that a man by the name of Henry Viable, "who was convicted from Norwich about 20 years since," had become a large and successful merchant with a fleet of 25 sailing ships trading to all parts of the world. Shades of Henry Cabell, perhaps (see Marking out the Space).

In 1994 a 10ft obelisk was unveiled in Calais in memory of Nelson's mistress, Lady Hamilton, who died in 1815. It had been paid for by an American member of the 1805 Club, formed to promote all things Nelsonian. In 1782, Cheshire-born Emma became a nursemaid in London where she was quickly embroiled in a series of amorous escapades before marrying Sir William Hamilton, British ambassador in Naples, in 1791. She first met Nelson in 1793 and their child, Horatia, was born eight years later. Hamilton died in 1803 and Nelson in 1805, and although Emma was left money by both it was frittered away. In 1813, shortly before fleeing to Calais, she was imprisoned for debt. Emma was said to have been remarkably beautiful - George Romney's many paintings of her confirm this - and she was only 53 when she died. Her early London life was clouded in scandals and whispers. She had several lovers, and in Wimbledon performed her "attitudes," in which she posed as well-known classical figures. After world war two, one local writer researching the history of Norwich hostelries asserted she was also known as Emma Hart, the shapely young lady who, clad in diaphanous veils, called herself "The Goddess of Love" and assisted the quack Doctor Graham in his "Temple of Health" lectures on the propagation of the species and the art and joys of the marriage bed. And extremely popular the lectures were, too. What is more, he claimed the duo appeared at the Great Room at the Maid's Head in Norwich, attracting a great crowd. Graham, who also had a "Celestial Bed" which he apparently hired out to childless couples, also died in poverty.

Luke Hansard (1752-1828), baptised at St Mary, Coslany, learned the printing trade in Norwich and went to London to print the Journals of the House of Commons. The publication still bears his name.

Heacham was the home of John Rolfe (1585-1622), one of the early Virginia settlers and one of the first men to experiment in growing tobacco. Rolfe was a member of a group led by Capt John Smith, and there is a story that during a series of warring episodes with the Powhatan Indians his life was saved by Princess Pocahontas. In 1613 (see Marking out the Space), Pocahontas married John Rolfe and came to England. Alas, Pocahontas died at Gravesend in 1617, leaving a son. Thus the story which is nurtured locally. But a 1991 book ("The Conquest of Paradise," by Kirkpatrick Sale, Hodder & Stoughton) tells a slightly different tale. In the first place, argued Mr Sale, Pocahontas was not a real princess; she was simply a daughter of the Powhatan chief Wahunseneka. And the bonds of marriage merely sealed a truce between the Powhatan and the settlers. Most tellingly, he said, her real name was not Pocahontas but Matoakah. Pocahontas was evidently her nickname, meaning wanton, teasing, or worse. According to Mr Sale the flirtatious Matoakah was only 12 or 13 when she first met English settlers in 1608 and when she was already known by her nickname. Rolfe is evidently on record as telling the authorities he wanted to marry her not out of "the unbridled desire of carnall affection," but for the good of the plantation, the honour of the country, and to convert "an unbelieving creature" to "the true knowledge."

The Vicar of Hell was a name playfully given by Henry V111 to John Skelton, his "poet laureate," perhaps because Skelton was rector of Diss - the pun being on Dis (Pluto, the Roman god of the nether regions, or the Greek Hades). Even Milton referred to it in his Areopagitica. Skelton became tutor to Prince Henry, later Henry V111, but he clashed with various bishops and took sanctuary at Westminster.

First recorded winner of the Dunmow Flitch (at Little Dunmow, Essex) in 1445 was a certain Richard Wright of Bawburgh - and his wife, presumably. The custom probably originated at the Dunmow church (then a priory) in an effort to encourage good relationships in marriage.

The first "nosey parker" is thought to have been Archbishop Matthew Parker, born Norwich 1504 and educated at Norwich Grammar School, who was known to be excessively inquisitive. He was appointed Archbishop of Canterbury in 1559, and died in 1575.

Queen Anne, daughter of King Wenceslas of Bohemia and the wife of Richard 11, is said to have introduced the fashion of riding side-saddle to the good ladies of Norwich. She evidently rode side-saddle in Norwich during the Royal visit of 1383. Hitherto, ladies invariably rode astride, as men still do.

In 1154 Nicholas Breakspear became Pope Adrian IV, the only Englishman ever to have become Pope. Most sources say he hailed from King's Langley, Hertfordshire, but a marshland tradition suggests he "once held the living" at Tydd St Mary. If so, the story presumably relates to some earlier church than the present building in the village.

The role of Sheriff dates to Saxon times and with ecclesiastical appointments is, in England, second only to the Crown in terms of antiquity. Norfolk's Sheriff is appointed by the sovereign, the successful name being "pricked" by a bodkin. Incidentally, Freemen of Norwich emerged during the 12th and 13th centuries, but not until the 13th century were records kept. Today, the title is held by about 600 people and is often passed from father to son.

5: People at Work

The earliest known industrial complex in Norfolk is Grimes Graves, the Neolithic flint mines near Brandon (Suffolk). Worked in phases between 2100BC and 1000BC, it represents the first systematic exploitation of flint reserves, the site covering some 90 acres and embracing about 360 shafts. Fingerprints of some of the early miners have been found impressed on chalk and on antler picks.

There are slight survivals of old ridge and furrow farming methods (blocks of field strips, called furlongs) at, among other places, Ryston and Hilgay, but they are difficult to recognise and the system was probably much more widespread than realised. There is also a curious grid of roads and fields, possibly Roman, aligned on the Peddars Way at Holme next Sea. And fragments of hedgerows and field patterns in the Elmhams and Ilketshalls, near Bungay (Suffolk), and in the Scole, Tivetshall, Diss and Long Stratton areas, may represent Roman or in some cases pre-Roman landscapes. Near Long Stratton and Dickleburgh, for example, the Roman road looks as though it was imposed on an older landscape.

In recent years many arable farmers have moved away from cereal growing. Some have switched to growing durum wheat, an ingredient of pasta foods like spaghetti. Some have tried deer rearing or converting their land into golf courses. Fish farms, camp sites and war games areas have also appeared. Even gourmet snail fattening has been put on the agenda. A very few switched to poppies. Trials of opium poppies (papaver somniferum, of low morphine content) began at two "secret" sites in 1986 with the co-operation of the Home Office. These were the Marianne (blue and white) variety. Some poppy seeds are used by the bakery industry, but the real purpose of the trials was to see if they could be used to produce high quality oils.

The University of East Anglia's rural technology unit of the School of Development Studies, which studies low-tech farming methods for Third World countries, used to use oxen for ploughing. They were Gunder and Frank, a pair of cross-bred Hereford-Friesian oxen.

Peter Boardman, of How Hill Farm, near Ludham, is thought to be Britain's only holly farmer. His father planted the trees in 1938/39. Caley Mill at Heacham is England's last remaining lavender farm. It is also home to the national collection of lavenders. In 1988, lavender bushes were sent to Virginia, USA, to mark the 374th anniversary of the marriage of Heacham-born John Rolfe to Pocahontas (see Figures in the Landscape).

The Bird's Eye fish finger, now an integral part of the English diet, first saw light of day in a joint Lowestoft-Yamouth factory operation in 1955. The first 1000 packets were made up in Yarmouth, where scores of different crumbs were tried for colour and different oils and batter tested to produce the right format. At the company's annual sales conference at Brighton that year one session was devoted to the launch of the new product, which had evidently been sold in two test areas with considerable success. Salesmen were told the selling points included: "No bones, no waste, no fuss." On launch, six fish fingers cost 1s 8d.

The area also had a major hand in the production of another large portion of the English stable diet, the baked bean. One North Walsham plant churned out half a million cans a day. Many of the beans came from America, but the British are thought to eat around 10 per cent of the world's annual consumption. Baked beans are actually dry white harricot beans or navy beans.

The world's biggest bacon slicing and packing plant is at Thetford. Tulip International, which sells meat products in 130 countries, handles an average of 25 lorryloads of bacon every day.

It takes the pea, on average, 2hr 30min from being harvested in the field to being frozen and packed at Lowestoft's Bird's Eye factory. Peas evidently account for 45 per cent of the nation's frozen green vegetable consumption. Crops have to be grown within 90-minute road journey of the factory, and during the busy six or seven-week season lorries will rush more than 50,000 tonnes to Lowestoft. It is planned like a military operation. Peas are tested by a "tenderometer" and frozen to minus 18degC. A team of pea gourmets check and taste each batch.

In 1990, at Gateshead garden festival, Bernard Lavery, of Terrington St Clement, smashed three world records for vegetable growing, including 46lb of celery. He already held the world record for a 124lb cabbage, a 28oz radish, a 108lb marrow and a 64lb courgette.

Cantley beet sugar factory, built by Dutchman Jerald van Rossum in 1912, was the first such complex in the country. In its first season the company processed 21,000 tonnes of beet, an amount now processed every few days. Purely as an aside, Cantley factory is one of the furthest identifiable objects to be seen on a clear day from the battlements of Norwich Castle - the distance being about 11 miles.

Perhaps the most famous chocolate product made in Norwich is the Yorkie bar. The automated line can handle 19,000 packs a day, each pack containing 24 bars.

Aldous ice cream has been in business in Norwich since the 1920s, when the family sold it from a barrow. And Augie Parravani, of Ellingham, who retired in 1986, had been making Parravani ice cream in the Waveney area for over 60 years.

Insurance giant Norwich Union, based in Norwich, reached its staffing zenith in the late 1980s when it had over 6500 workers on its books in Norfolk alone. In 1989, Norwich Union claimed its canteens provided more midday meals than anyone else in the city.

There were 18 rather unusual lavatories at Jeyes factory, Thetford. The flushing was controlled by computer. Moreover, they were flushed automatically every few minutes. The lavatories, which sat side by side in the same room, were used for testing toilet cleansing chemicals. The computer saves a great deal of chain pulling.

Norfolk's most efficient "nose" is at Weybourne. An atmosphere observatory built in a former war-time pillbox, it is part of a six-nation global network of centres with equipment so sensitive they can detect the faintest whiff of pollution. The Weybourne complex is said to be able to detect a passing car or boat, or even if the North Norfolk Railway is running to time.

An Ascarid is an intestinal worm. It was also the name of the mole machine used to bore a 2.2km sewerage outlet under the North Sea from West Runton. This Ascarid weighed 44 tonnes and travelled up to 25m a day digging its own grave, for the machine was to be sealed in when the tunnel was complete.

Possibly the heaviest pub sign in Norfolk, at the Coachmakers, in Norwich.

Bircham Newton construction industry training centre, established in 1966 on 450 acres of former airfield, became the largest of its kind in the world. And Fakenham has England's only surviving example of a town gas works, which supplied gas between 1825 and 1965. It is now a museum.

Talking of construction, Norwich's city walls were completed in 1343 after nearly 50 years in the making. And in 1939, corporation bricklayer Harry Loveday was given the job of bricking up the civic regalia in a special vault in the Guildhall dungeon. After the war, Harry was also given the job of digging it out again.

Tom Smith's Norwich cracker factory has long supplied Christmas entertainments to the Royal household at Sandringham. In 1988, however, their crackers went further afield, to the White House, where they adorned the Presidential table of Ronald Reagan.

Wymondham may be home to the county's oldest law firm. There are records of an attorney named Thomas Seaborne dealing with the Town Charity in 1660. The law firm concerned is now known as Pomeroy & Son, but there is a direct and documented line from 1660.

Norwich provision market, once upon a time much larger than it is now, was created by the Normans and has thus been in operation for 900 years. It is one of the largest and oldest open air markets in the country.

The heaviest pub sign in Norfolk, weighing just short of a ton, is probably that of the Coachmakers, in St Stephens, Norwich. It was made in 1937 by an Italian who shaped wet concrete from a bucket. The sign scene, still fixed to the wall of the pub, was taken from a 1791 print and depicts the former St Stephen's Gate and a cavalier. The largest pub sign was erected in 1655 outside the White Hart Inn at Scole. It cost more than £1000 and spanned the road to Norwich. Although it disappeared over 200 years ago, prints and records show it carried 25 lifesize figures including lions, Jonah emerging from a whale's mouth, Neptune, and an astronomer. It also carried coats of arms, including those of James Peck, who was landlord at the time.

Roys (Wroxham) Ltd, opened in 1895, claimed to be the "largest village store in the world." The store is also thought to have had one of the first wireless sets in the area. Possibly the county's smallest shop was opened by Millie Wright in 1969. She converted the entrance hall of her home in Queen's Square, Attleborough, into an antiques shop. Floor space measured roughly one and a quarter yards by two and a quarter yards.

Construction of Bacton gas terminal began in 1968. Gas is pumped to the terminal from the drilling platforms in 75cm diameter undersea pipes. From the complex, more pipes spread in three branches, taking supplies towards Leicester and the Midlands, towards Cambridge, and towards London. Current undersea gas fields feeding into Bacton include Barque, Sole Pit, Clipper, Galleon, Leman, Indefatigable, and Sean North and South.

At the turn of the century George Rook, of Cromer, came ashore from the lifeboat one day and complained of a bad back. A friend offered a remedy and wrote down the details. Mr Rook took it to a Church Street chemist, and in due course it became known as Rook's Drops. It actually contained sweet spirit of nitre, tincture of red lavender, Friar's balsam, salvolatile and rectified terebene, a few drops being taken on sugar. It was reported to taste awful. Even so, a few years ago I was told an occasional bottle still sold.

A powder treatment for horses to improve condition and appetite and invented by a Diss veterinary surgeon 150 years ago also stood the test of time. The ingredients were kept secret, but in 1984 it was reported that production of Cuppiss' Constitution Powders was being affected by the poor harvest of a certain West African root. The powder originated with Francis Cuppiss, who retired to The Wilderness, Diss, in 1874 after 50 years as chemist and vet in Mere Street.

Cromer lighthouse was established in 1719, but the present tower was built in 1833. Its 1500-watt light can be seen for 20 miles out to sea. To further aid shipping, there is the Trinity House automated light vessel Dudgeon, the Lanby or light float Newarp, and the Dowsing automated lighthouse. One of the best known light vessels was Smith's Knoll, off Yarmouth, but it was dropped from shipping forecasts in 1993.

There are hundreds of wrecks waiting to be found and explored, a number of them submarines. One incident occurred on the night of July 4, 1909. A flotilla of eight submarines, three torpedo boats and a parent ship, the Bonadventure, was heading south. In darkness and thick fog some four miles north-west of the Haisbro' light off Cromer, the steamship Eddystone, from Gibraltar bound for Hull with a cargo of barley, ran over submarine C11, which sank. Most of the crew was lost. Submarine C17 was also damaged.

Happisburgh lighthouse has been a Norfolk landmark since 1791, having been completed five years after a severe storm evidently sank 70 ships and drowned 600 men off Norfolk. Its distinctive red and white bands were first painted in 1883, but from 1929 it had no full-time lightkeeper and from 1942 was powered by electricity. About a month before Trinity House was due to close it in 1988 a local petition won a stay of execution. A lighthouse trust was formed and a donation of £15,000 enabled a Private Bill to pass through Parliament which finally received Royal Assent in 1989. In 1990 the Queen Mother visited the lighthouse, and its bicentenary was celebrated in 1991. The Happisburgh Lighthouse Trust is now a private lighthouse trust with power to keep the light burning.

Stiffkey men once had the reputation of letting the women do most of the hard work. One turn-of-the-century writer, passing through, said he saw a few "unkept loafers." But, he added, it was a fact that many of the women of Stiffkey "are mainly responsible for the maintenance of the homes and families," by back-breakingly gathering cockles on the ebb tide and carrying them back to the village prior to transportation to King's Lynn market.

Richards' shipyard in Lowestoft built the Nivaga 11, a passenger and cargo boat for the south-west Pacific islands of Tuvalu. She was launched by the Princess Royal in 1988, watched by Tuvalu's prime minister, Dr Tomasi Puapua, and his wife, Riana. Nivaga 11 is used to ferry children to school, transport food and take patients to hospital. In 1989, a first day postal cover issued by Tuvalu charted the islands' links with Lowestoft, and the vessel appeared on the stamp. And descendants of the mutineers of HMS Bounty have a lifeline to the outside world thanks to George Prior Engineering, also of Lowestoft. This yard built a 40ft vessel equipped with engines, oars and sail, which Pitcairn islanders use to ply backwards and forwards through the rough surf to collect goods and supplies from visiting ships.

The oldest Broads' boating holiday firm is thought to be Blakes, which started business over 80 years ago renting out wherry yachts. History was made on Wroxham Broad in 1987 when five wherries - Olive, Lady Edith, Solace, Hathor and Albion - sailed together for the first time in 40 years. White Moth and Maud were being restored at the time. Many other wherries ended their days as unwanted hulks left to rot in various waterways and Broads. A few years ago the remains of a Norfolk keel, the last of many which were the river workhorses for decades before the wherries, was dug out of a bank of the river Yare at Whitlingham, where it had been buried for 90 years. The keel, originally the Dee-Dah, carried cargo on the Yare, and at the end of its working life it was used as a bank strengthener. The last time I saw the remains they were stored under sheeting beside the river in King Street, Norwich.

A Yarmouth link with the Royal Navy was severed when the sixth HMS Yarmouth, a veteran frigate also known as Crazy Y, was decommissioned and subsequently deliberately sunk during target practice. According to the Navy it was a great honour for a ship to be used for target practice rather than be broken up for scrap. Crazy Y's framed Freedom of the Borough scroll was handed back to Yarmouth to be retained and then handed to No 7. HMS Lowestoft, a Rothesey-class frigate, suffered a similar "honour" when she ended her days as a North Atlantic target for a new type of torpedo. The latest HMS Norfolk, a £150 million Type-3 frigate, and the sixth Royal Navy ship to bear the Norfolk name, was launched at Portland Naval base, Dorset, in 1990.

When the captain and members of the crew of the minesweeper HMS Brinton visited the village of Brinton for a reception in 1987, she was the oldest ship in the Navy, having been launched in 1952. In the 1960s, members of the crew of the minesweeper HMS Yaxham were occasional visitors to Yaxham for darts and cricket matches.

In 1888, the paddle steamer Victoria, bound for Yarmouth and packed with holiday trippers, grounded on Church Rock, a pile of stones some 400m offshore at Cromer and believed by many to be the remains of the church of St Peter, Shipden, a village long vanished beneath the waves. Fortunately for the passengers, the accident was spotted by local fishermen who put to sea at once. Everyone was rescued and the wreck of the Victoria was later blown up. This is the only known instance of a ship being sunk by a church.

A 50-year-old motor torpedo boat, MTB 102, was bought by Brundall and Blofield Sea Scouts in the 1970s. She was originally purchased by the Admiralty in 1937 and saw service mainly in the Channel. She was the third last warship away from Dunkirk.

Kit is a Lowestoft term for a fish container holding about 10st. Previously, the old herring measure was the cran, about 28st. The cran followed the much older measure of the long hundred. Shrimps are measured by the peck or bushel, and crabs by the ped. There are also local name variations. At Yarmouth a flounder is known as a fluke, while at Lowestoft it is a butt. At Lowestoft, a seabed obstruction is a heft, while at Yarmouth it is a snag. The type of crab pot used by Cromer fishermen today is thought to have been introduced 200 years ago from Yorkshire by a man named Stanford. They vary only slightly from the original design.

Caister volunteer lifeboat service is the only privately-run lifeboat in the country. The station has a long and distinguished history, having been on duty for more than 130 years. Caister became a national interest in 1901 after nine of the crew drowned when waves swamped their boat, the Beauchamp. The oft-repeated phrase, "Caister men never turn back," was said to have been coined by a member of the Haylett family at the inquest. But he never said it. At least, not quite like that.

Henry Blogg was a member of the Cromer lifeboat crew for 53 years and won more awards than any other lifeboatman, including three RNLI gold medals. During Blogg's reign the Cromer boat went out 387 times and saved 873 lives. In 1988, Sheringham marked 150 years of local lifeboats since the launch in 1838 of the town's first boat, the 33ft oar-powered Augusta. Bits of the hulk of the Augusta were hauled from Ranworth Broad in time for display during the anniversary celebrations.

A new 1987 Lowestoft racing yacht, the 25ft Merganser, became the first Broads' one-design brown boat to be built in glass fibre, and the first to be built for nearly 50 years. Only 31 brown boats were built between the turn of the century and the 1930s. Pintail (No 29) was destroyed by fire at Oulton Broad (Suffolk), and Dotterel (No 8) is said to have perished in a hurricane in Montego Bay in the 1950s.

In 1983 there was news of two old Lowestoft boats left to their fate in a faraway graveyard in the Falkland Islands. Both steam drifters, they were the Golden Chance (LT 371) and the Afterglow, built during world war one. Both were reported beached near Port Stanley.

Lowestoft's Armada Post at the entrance to Martin's Score in the High Street has been preserved since 1688. The post bears the initials "TM" and the dates 1688, 1788 and 1888. The numerals indicate restorations. The initials are thought to be those of Thomas Meldrum who sent his ship, the Elizabeth, to fight the Armada.

Caister lifeboat station, the only privately run lifeboat in the country.

The memorial in Clement Court, Norwich, commemorating the first English provincial newspaper.

Norfolk's first railway lines were the Yarmouth to Norwich (1844) and Norwich to Brandon (1845). By 1906 the county system was largely complete, with Blakeney the only community of size more than five miles from a station. Berney Arms, on the Reedham to Yarmouth line, may be the smallest and loneliest rail halt in Norfolk, for it is one of the few rail stops in the country to be without a road link. Close to the banks of Breydon on Halvergate Marsh; it is a favourite stop for birdwatchers. For many years drivers on the Norwich to Liverpool Street run had to deal with "The Throat," the bit just outside Liverpool Street where grimy city walls closed in on either side and passengers reached for their coats and bags. The problem was that trains coming into and departing from the station's 18 platforms had to take their turn to squeeze through a narrow channel only three lines wide. And by the way, beside the track at Bentley, between Ipswich and Manningtree, was a tiny marker which signified the passing of trains from Norwich control to Liverpool Street control, or vice versa.

When British Rail announced it was to scrap its restaurant on the Fenman service from King's Lynn to London it caused a bit of a stir because the train was often used by Royalty. Regular passengers fondly recalled the day in 1986 when the train broke down and the Queen's breakfast had to be carried along the platform to her carriage.

Passenger complaints at London's Liverpool Street station in the 1980s included the fact that the arrivals board occasionally showed trains due in on platform 19. There was no platform 19. British Rail finally explained that when a train had not had been allocated a particular platform the computer automatically marked it up for No 19. And BR's £4million Trowse rail river bridge, opened in 1987 just outside Norwich station, was said at the time to be the only one in the country capable of carrying 25,000 volt overhead cables. Still with trains, the four-mile stretch of the Wells to Walsingham line is the world's longest ten-and-a-quarter inch gauge railway. Opened in 1982, it received a new engine in 1986, named the Norfolk Hero, built with a water tender at each end to give added power on the inclines.

The first cottage hospital in England is said to have been Shotesham Infirmary, founded in the first half of the 18th century by William Fellowes (1706-75). It was built for the use of the apothecary surgeon to the village, Benjamin Gooch, one of the country's leading provincial surgeons. Britain's first industrial nurse may have been Philippa Flowerday, who was trained at the Norfolk and Norwich Hospital in 1876 along lines originally recommended by Florence Nightingale, and who was appointed as nurse to J & J Colman's Carrow Works in 1878.

Sir Roger Le Strange, of Hunstanton, became Surveyor of the Imprimery (in effect, the Press), established in 1660 to curb printing abuses. He took over the post in 1663 and took under his wing all the printing offices in England, as well as the vendors of books and papers. He published and wrote the Intelligencer (1663-1666) and The Newes, and helped found the City Mercury newspaper in 1675 and the Observator in 1681. He lost his post in 1688-89, died in 1704, and was buried at St Giles-in-the-Fields. The first ever provincial newspaper, the Norwich Post, was founded in 1701 at a spot near Clement Court (a name close to my own heart) in Redwell Street. It was followed by the Norwich Gazette and the Postman (both 1706) and the Norwich Courant (1714).

The late Jack Murton, of Tittleshall, delivered newspapers for 72 years, beginning on the day world war one broke out. At one time he had a 45-mile round through Beeston, Litcham, Great Dunham, the Lexhams, Mileham, Tittleshall, Wellingham and Longham.

Norfolk has inherited a great deal of the paraphernalia of war - pillboxes, bunkers, army camps, gun emplacements, dumps, depots, firing ranges and airfields. Militarily, the area has been useful and vulnerable for centuries. One of the most vulnerable areas, according to tradition, is Weybourne, where deep-water ships can manoeuvre close to the shoreline. At the time of the Armada, Weybourne was heavily defended with men, horses, earthworks and ordinances. Even today it is home to a mobile radar tracking station.

Reminders of war - the crumbling remains of Wendling air base's bomb dump, now overgrown and half hidden by greenery in Honeypot Wood.

The litter of war is forever turning up, the most usual items being grenades, flares, ammunition of all kinds, unexploded bombs and mines. They are dredged out of rivers, caught in nets at sea, found in caches and uncovered on beaches. At one stage, Lowestoft's inshore fleet fishermen were averaging over 15 mines or bombs a year.

Stanford troop training area, which absorbs many acres of Breckland also, perversely, helps to preserve much of its ancient landscape. It was in the Brecks in about 1915 that some of the first tanks were tested and approved prior to shipment to the Somme in 1916. King George V is said to have watched trials of experimental "land ships" near Thetford in 1915, and the following year crews were trained - again in secret - at Canada Farm, Thetford. For many years, incidentally, the battle area retained the services of a single tank, used by aircraft as a target on night-time reconnaisance missions. It was said to have been the most photographed tank in Europe.

Norfolk's most decorated soldier was Harry Cator, of Sprowston, who won the VC at Arras in 1917. He had already been awarded the Military Medal and the French Croix de Guerre. Czechoslovakian world war two hero Joe Capka is buried at Easton.

During the last war Holkham Hall was occupied by the military, largely for training purposes. The names of tanks - Anson, Atlas, Albatross, Albacore, Albemarle - were painted above their parking places on the wall of the kitchen court. In the years immediately following the war many Axis prisoners and Allied supporters were camped in the county. There were Poles in Breckland, Italians around Dereham, Ukrainians in King's Lynn, and Germans and Czechs in the Fens.

Members of the 1st Battalion, Royal Norfolk Regiment DV Club for officers who served between D-Day and VE-Day, have met for regular reunions since 1945. In 1986, members of the Norwich branch of the Desert Rats travelled to Germany for a reconciliation with German members of the Afrika Corps, in Baiersbronn in the Black Forest. They had fought against each other in the North African campaign.

A group called Trace, or the Trans-Atlantic Children's Enterprise, came into being in 1985 specifically to help the children of world war two American Servicemen and British mothers find their fathers. It was said at the time that the number of offspring by American Servicemen in this country may have been as high as 22,000. In its first year of operation, Trace helped arrange 11 reunions between war children and their fathers.

The travel guide which inadvertently lent its name to a series of raids by German bombers on Norwich and other historic cities, has latterly been printed locally. The bombing campaign became known as the Baedeker Raids, and in 1987 Jarrolds of Norwich acquired the worldwide English rights to print the current versions.

Norfolk's first recorded tethered flight was made in January, 1784, by James Bunn, who launched a 10ft balloon in the Pantheon, an entertainments building in Spring Gardens, Norwich. The first recorded local unpiloted free flight was on February 16, 1784, when a 5ft balloon was released from Quantrell's Public Gardens, Norwich. Watched by hundreds of spectators, it drifted towards Wymondham. The first person to make a free flight in Norfolk was James Deeker, who made an ascent in a gas-filled balloon from Quantrell's Gardens on June 1, 1785. After a 10-mile flight he came down in a meadow at Sisland. Three weeks' later, on June 22, he had a second flight. Striking trees on take-off, he nevertheless stayed in the air for 12 miles before landing at Topcroft. The first woman to fly locally was probably a Mrs Graham, who in 1825 ascended in a gas balloon with Col John Harvey, of Thorpe Lodge, from a spot in Bracondale. First local aircraft take-off and landing is thought to have been at Snarehill, Thetford, in 1911. It was probably a Bleriot B2 belonging to the Aeroplane Company, Royal Engineers. Normally based at Farnborough, a number of Bleriots were taken to Snarehill in 1911 for summer manoeuvres. One of the first pilots to demonstrate flying locally, in 1912, was B C Hucks, whose appearances drew enormous crowds. Incidentally, calculations over the last few years suggest that Norfolk has had over 250 landing fields - and several hundred crashes.

At 4.40am on July 10, 1940, three Spitfires of 66 Squadron (Robertson, Cooke and Studd) took off from RAF Coltishall. Thirty minutes later a German bomber fomation was spotted, and 20 miles east of Winterton Sgt Robertson shot down a Dornier 17. It crashed into the sea and the two-man crew was lost. That same day the Luftwaffe lost 19 planes shot down or damaged, and the RAF in general lost seven; but Robertson's success was subsequently acknowledged as one of the opening shots of the Battle of Britain. Early next morning, July 11, Sqdn Ldr Douglas Bader, of 242 Squadron also based at Coltishall, in a Hurricane, shot down a Dornier 17 off Cromer. A Spitfire flown by Sqdn Ldr Leigh was hit in the oil tank south-east of Yarmouth, but landed safely.

And pigs really did fly. At least, the Pulham Pigs did. An airship station was developed there during world war one. The base was heavily involved in flying operations during and after the war, and many famous airships visited or were stationed there. In 1925, R33 broke from her moorings in gale force winds and still with a skeleton crew on board, and it was 29 hours before they were able to land. The ill-fated R101, which crashed in France in 1930, also had close links with Pulham. Another famous incident was in 1919 when R34 became the first airship to make the round voyage between Britain and America. She left Scotland at 2.42am on July 2, reached Mineola, Long Island, at 2pm on July 6, left at 5.51am on July 10 and reached Pulham again at 7.56am on July 13.

On the subject of balloons, the Meteorological Office station at Hemsby every day launches four hydrogen-filled balloons to measure temperature, humidity and pressure. They are said to rise some 30km into the atmosphere. Nine out of 10 evidently come down in the sea.

A Zeppelin raid on Yarmouth during the early months of world war one was the first recorded aerial bombing attack on civilians in this country. And a direct hit by a German bomber on a hostel which stood near the present Palm Court Hotel, Yarmouth, on May 11, 1943, killed 26 women members of the Auxiliary Territorial Army (ATS), the biggest loss of life sustained in one blow by any of the women's services.

The first publicly-known panic over an A-bomb incident in this area occurred in 1956 when a Stratojet crash set fire to the bomb store at RAF Lakenheath. Disaster was averted. Two years later there were two incidents at RAF Sculthorpe. In one, an American sergeant threatened to commit suicide by firing pistol shots into a stockpile of A-bombs. Then, so it was said, a bomber landed with a faulty release catch and a bomb tilting at an alarming angle only 3ft above the runway. Valiant bomber Xd818, which underwent restoration at RAF Marham in 1982, had its moments, too. It was this aircraft which on May 15, 1957, dropped the first hydrogen bomb at the Christmas Island test site.

Lakenheath and Mildenhall (both Suffolk) are known as American bases, but in reality they are leased. Thus they are still correctly known as RAF Lakenheath and RAF Mildenhall. They fly the Union Jack alongside the Stars and Stripes, and have British liaison officers. Lakenheath, a front-line fighter-bomber station, is known locally as "Little America." The dollar is base currency, the New York Times sits on the news stands beside the local papers, and American kids with Norfolk accents play soccer. Mildenhall is a huge transportation base, carting personnel, stores and equipment between the States, Britain and Europe. The huge freight hall has a British customs post.

Mildenhall has also been home to two of the world's most secret aircraft, the Cold War U-2 spy plane and SR-71, otherwise known as Blackbird. The existence locally of U-2s was repeatedly denied by British and American authorities, but its presence at local airfields was regularly logged by aircraft spotters. So too Blackbird. For 15 years or so this remarkable edge-of-space surveillance plane, the fastest in the world at mach-3, or 2200mph, did not exist at Mildenhall, either. But aviation buffs and members of the public logged sightings so regularly that eventually the authorities relented. Before the last one returned to America in 1990, Blackbird had become a favourite static and flying exhibit at Mildenhall air shows.

British airmen flying out of the former American base at RAF Sculthorpe undertook secret Cold War surveillance missions. Computer and radar screen operators at RAF Neatishead also played a key role throughout the Cold War period. They could take in at a glance representations (on screen, they looked like coloured tadpoles - green for Nato, red for non-Nato) of aircraft circling Schipol airport, Amsterdam, jets climbing to altitude on the Polar route to the States, Russian civilian airliners on landing approach at Heathrow, and Russian military aircraft on patrol between Scotland and the Faroes. In fact, almost everything in the air around Britain, and all at once. A few years ago it used to be said that, if they did ever spot inbound aggressive aircraft, then Neatishead's survival time was limited. It was calculated they had about four minutes to raise the alarm before they would be eliminated.

The Holbeach (Lincolnshire) firing range near Gedney Drove End covers about three square miles of The Puff, Mare Tail and Blue Back sands in the Wash, and innumerable saltmarsh targets for visiting aircraft to bombard, including three red painted vessels moored in shallow water, one an old lighter and another a former minesweeper. The Royal Navy used to be brought in to patch up the holes now and again, just to keep the vessels upright so they could be shot at again.

Wing Cmdr Ken Wallis, of Reymerston, a stout champion of the autogyro, became a familiar figure at fetes and gatherings, thrilling crowds with his flying machines. He began building autogyros at Reymerston in 1964 and over the years set many world records, including an altitude record of 18,516ft.

6: Simple Diversions

Mother Julian of Norwich, who lived from about 1373 to 1416 in an anchorage attached to the church of St Julian and St Edward in Norwich, wrote her "Revelations of Divine Love" in circa 1413. It is the earliest known book in English written by a woman. Another mystic, the extraordinary Margery Kempe, of King's Lynn, was born about 1373. She met Mother Julian at least once and had completed an autobiographical account of her pilgrimages by 1436. Her book is the first known autobiography by a woman. In 1980 "The Book of Margery Kempe" was bought by the British Museum for £50,000.

One of the earliest known Valentine's Day messages was from Norfolk. It was in the form of a love letter from Margery Brews to John Paston, a member of the famous family of letters. Dated February 14, 1477, it reflected the writer's anguish as various parents argued over the dowry: "But if you love me, as I hope that indeed you do, you will not leave me because of it; if you did not have half the estates you have, I would not forsake you, even if I had to work as hard as any woman alive. . . I beseech you that this letter be not seen by any earthly creature save only yourself. And this letter was written at Topcroft with a very sad heart. By your own M B." Happily, they married later that same year.

Tucked away on the extensive shelving of the Norfolk Record Office, in the air conditioned safety of an underground strongroom, are many treasures. Diaries, deeds, records, rolls, maps and manuscripts. Rider Haggard's "King Solomon's Mines," "She" and "Cleopatra," all in his own hand. A few chapters of George Borrow's "Wild Wales." R H Mottram's "Spanish Farm." And one of the oldest of the lot, the 12th century Norwich charter. In all, the Norwich strongroom holds well over two million documents.

Ebenezer Cobham Brewer's "Dictionary of Fact and Fable," first published in 1870, is still going strong. Brewer, born 1810, was the son of two Norwich schoolteachers at Mile End House. He became a priest, a teacher, lived for a time in Paris, and then began to write mainly educational books.

Many fictional characters had their roots in Norfolk. Capt W E Johns, author of the "Biggles" sagas of the air, was stationed at RAF Narborough during world war one. Indeed, he is said to have been one of the first officers to have flown from Narborough, which is given an honourable mention in "Biggles of the Camel Corps." And "Thomas the Tank Engine" was created many years ago by the Rev Wilbert Awdry, who had a living at Wisbech during the time when the Wisbech-Upwell tramway was runnning. As for 1950s radio hero and crime-buster Dick Barton, his scriptwriters once let slip that the special agent was educated at Norwich School.

Charles Dickens visited Yarmouth in 1848, staying at the Royal Hotel. Later that year the monthly serialisation of "David Copperfield" began, containing lots of references to Yarmouth and leaving in its wake many heated arguments, particularly as to the manner and siting of Mr Peggoty's home, visualised as an upturned boat.

One of our greatest comic writers, Pelham Grenville Wodehouse, was a regular visitor to the Le Strange family's Hunstanton Hall in the 1920s, and indeed, his wife was a King's Lynn lady. P G often sat typing in a punt on the lake at the Hall, and his books are littered with Norfolk references and connections. His London address for many years was Norfolk Street.

The church of St Julian, and the reconstructed Julian cell, can be found in Norwich.

Sherlock Holmes fans will be pleased to learn that Sir Arthur Conan Doyle was also a visitor to Norfolk. His story of the "Hound of the Baskervilles" is thought to have been hatched around the fireside in a Cromer hotel in 1901 while Conan Doyle was spending a pleasant hour with his golfing friend, Fletcher Robinson. One theory is that the black hound was inspired by legends of North Norfolk's Black Shuck. What is known is that Robinson's coachman was one Henry Baskerville. And "The Dancing Men" was set near North Walsham. It was written in 1903 while Conan Doyle was staying at Happisburgh.

James Pattinson, of East Harling, has been one of Norfolk's most prolific writers over the last few years. He began writing on board ship during world war two, and in 1993 happily corrected the proofs of his 90th novel.

In 1990, writer Iman Wilkens, in his book, "Where Troy Once Stood" (Rider), proposed that Homer's epics belonged not to Turkey or Greece, but to Europe - and to East Anglia in particular. Moreover, he suggested that the site of Troy was close to Cambridge; that the Fens were the Thracian Sea; that the Thymbre was the river Thet; that Caystrius was the river Yare near Norwich; and that King's Lynn was Lyrnessus, the home town of Achilles' girlfriend.

In October, 1993, a Norwich man wrote to the Eastern Daily Press to point out an error the paper had in its columns exactly 100 years before. In 1893, the EDP reported that Norwich Victoria had won the Great Eastern Railway first aid competition. The reference turned up again in the paper's "100 Years Ago" feature in 1993 - only this time a reader said the 1883 winners had actually been Norwich Thorpe.

In 1974, a new title appeared among lists of anthropological books published by a New York book firm. Taking its place alongside "The Dinka of the Sudan" and "The Ma'Anyan of Indonesian Borneo" was "Hennege: A Social System In Miniature." Hennege was the fictional name the author gave to a real village in darkest Norfolk - actually Thornage - and his studies dealt with the village and its people. Somewhat surprisingly, this academic work reached Norwich bookshops and caused a bit of a stir because it delved into social structures, rituals, values, schools, marriages, and so on. Names had been changed to protect the innocent, but villagers told me at the time it did not take much working out who was who.

In 1988 bookworms were invited to respond to a library amnesty for non-returned books. One book returned at King's Lynn had been "borrowed" for 42 years.

Ralph Vaughan Williams' ever popular "Fantasia on Greensleeves," written in 1929 for the opera "Sir John in Love," is said to include a Norfolk folk song called "Lovely Joan."

The village of Ansty in Wiltshire raised £10,000 for charity from an art auction in 1988, thanks largely to the pulling power of one Arthur C Carrick, alias the Prince of Wales, otherwise Prince Charles, who lent a watercolour, "Farm Building in Norfolk." When the picture was exhibited that same year at the Royal Academy summer exhibition it was signed simply "C 87" and was identified as a scene at Wood Farm, Wolferton, on the Royal estate. Another watercolour painted in Norfolk by the Prince of Wales, a landscape of Dersingham, was featured in a set of Royal Mail stamps issued in January, 1994. Paintings by Prince Charles were also included in the Burnham Market arts festival for a number of years.

When the Armada exhibition was held at Greenwich in 1988, Gaywood church lent two pictures. Said to have been painted on wood from Armada wrecks, the pictures, of Flemish origin, illustrated the Armada under sail and the story of Guy Fawkes. Both pictures dated from the time of Elizabeth 1.

The sculptor Henry Moore had a close connection with Wighton. He came to North Norfolk in the 1922 when his sister Mary was appointed school mistress at the local school. Indeed, he did some of his earliest work in the schoolhouse yard, having collected flints from the lanes and fields. He also had a married sister at Mulbarton and a brother at Stoke Ferry. Moore's father is buried at Wighton, and Henry, a student at the Royal College of Art, was a holiday visitor to the village over a number of years.

A certain amount of art was left behind in the wake of world war two. The Yanks flew most of their nose cone decoration back to the States, but a few murals still remain in remote and desolate airfield buildings. More unusually, the lounge, stair wall and bathroom of a house on Swanton Road, Dereham, was painted in 1945 by Angelo Previato, an Italian prisoner of war based at a local camp. The pictures ranged from a Regency hunting scene to cowboys, mountains, snow scenes, a cottage panorama, and cherubs.

The tonic sol fa system of writing music in a letter notation was first employed in teaching sight reading to children by Elizabeth Glover of Norwich. The system was supported by the Rev John Curwen with such enthusiasm that in 1863 he opened a Tonic Sol Fa College with offices in Finsbury Square, London.

Every year for a number of years Glenn Miller fan Sid Cullington, of Norwich, staged a one-man Miller memorial concert each December when, on the anniversary of the bandleader's disappearance over the Channel, he sat in a Norwich airport hangar - where the Miller band once appeared - and played a selection of Miller records.

Norwich's original theatre, opened in 1758, received the Royal assent through an Act of Parliament in 1768 and was the first outside London entitled to call itself Theatre Royal. When members of the Peking Opera visited the theatre in 1986 they ate their way though hundreds of bars of KitKat. In 1987 the cast of "Ruddigore" had to go outside and run round the back of the theatre to change costumes because the set was too big for the stage, leaving no room for exit right.

Players at Norwich's Maddermarket Theatre, one of the most famous amateur theatres in the country, still retain their anonymity. And the story of "Babes in the Wood" is derived from the tale of two children said to have been snatched from their home at Griston Hall and left to die in Wayland Woods, near Watton. Dan Leno made his Drury Lane debut in the show in 1888.

Sheringham Little Theatre houses one of the country's few remaining seaside repertory companies, and Cromer one of the last remaining pier companies. Yarmouth has one of only two permanent covered circus arenas in the UK, the local arena coming complete with a water spectacular.

In 1987 comedian Bradley Walsh, star of the Cromer pier show, was suddenly taken ill and hospitalised. At the next performance the audience was faced by an empty chair and a telephone on stage while they listened to Walsh cracking jokes by phone from his hospital bed.

The first public moving picture display in the county may have been the 1886 debut of "living pictures" at King's Lynn by showman Randall Williams. The first display in Norwich is thought to have been on January 11, 1897, at the Agricultural Hall, now Anglia TV. Then, Gilbert's Circus offered "the first appearance of the Royal Cinematographe," the "animated photographs" including a prizefight featuring Jem Mace and scenes on Yarmouth beach. In 1908 one of the first purpose-built cinemas, The Gem, opened at Yarmouth. The talkies came to Norwich at the Picture House in the Haymarket in February, 1929. It was the sixth cinema in England to install the Western Electric system, opening with Al Jolson in "The Singing Fool." The smallest local cinema was opened near Dereham. With room for a dozen viewers, it was named the Toftwood Playhouse and even had a miniature Wurlitzer.

Norfolk has played host to dozens of film and TV companies, and locations such as King's Lynn, Heydon, Thetford forest, Leziate gravel pits and the North Norfolk Railway have appeared regularly on screens. In the 1970s Melton Constable Hall, then empty, played host to Joseph Losey and the makers of "The Go-Between," when the female lead was Julie Christie. In the 1930s another star actually lived at the Hall. She was Madeleine Carroll, who married ex-Guardsman Philip Astley in 1931, though she later divorced him. Her Hollywood films included "The 39 Steps," "The Prisoner of Zenda," and "North West Mounted Police." During world war two she worked in a hospital in France and was awarded the Legion d'Honneur. Madeleine died a recluse in Marbella in 1987.

Lewis Ernest Watts Mills, otherwise Sir John Mills, once lived at Belton, where his father taught and where, because of schoolboy ribbing, he changed his name to Jack (rather than Lewis). Later he changed it again, to John. He made his stage debut at the Belton village institute, dancing a hornpipe accompanied by his sister Mabel, better known as Annette Mills; attended Sir John Leman School at Beccles, where he played Puck in a 1918 production of "A Midsummer Night's Dream"; attended Norwich High School for Boys in Upper St Giles and worked as a corn merchant in Ipswich. In the 1930s he had a football trial with Norwich City, but was not taken on, and so turned to the stage instead. Sir John was born in 1908 at the Watts Naval Training School - hence, presumably, the Christian name Watts - when his father was a member of staff there (see Marking out the Space).

In 1940 Michael Micklewhite, aged seven, from London, was evacuated with 13 other children to North Runcton. He lived at Church Farm and attended the local school from 1940 to 1945. In 1969, this time as Michael Caine the film star, he made a nostalgic return for a reunion with the family which had looked after him.

A number of famous Hollywood stars, including Walter Matthau, Glenn Miller and Clark Gable, visited or were stationed in the area during world war two. One of the most popular and the most modest was James Stewart. Once a Liberator pilot based at Tibenham and Old Buckenham, he held a special place in British and American hearts. In 1975 he paid the first of a couple of nostalgic visits to Tibenham, and in 1983 attended a 2nd Air Division reunion in Norfolk. At a banquet at the old Norwood Rooms in Aylsham Road, Norwich, during which he declined an offer to sit at the top table, he was finally persuaded to make a short speech. He thanked the Norwich people "who were so kind and thoughtful and encouraging 40 years ago," and recalled how he detested powdered egg. Indeed, he said, he came to feel that the man who had invented it "had a grouse against humanity." On mission days, however, they were given "two real eggs for breakfast from real Norfolk hens." Earlier, the star of dozens of films, including "The Glenn Miller Story," was dragged on to the stage to conduct the band through "Moonlight Serenade." It brought the house down.

During the last war the American Red Cross Service Club in Norwich kept a register containing the signatures of visitors. One 1944 signature read: Frank Sinatra. Probably a hoax, but stranger things happened.

In 1953 the new village hall at Sharrington, near Holt, was opened by members of the cast of the radio serial "The Archers." And in 1988 two members of the cast, Patricia Greene (Jill) and June Spencer (Peggy) went back to Sharrington to mark another stage of refurbishment.

King's Lynn mart (St Valentine's) and Downham Market (Winnold) open the local fair season, which ends with Norwich Christmas fair. The tradition of the Lynn and Downham fairs may be over 1000 years old. It was also at King's Lynn that Frederick Savage, the 19th century engineer, took fairs out of the Middle Ages by harnessing them to steam. Thurston's "living pictures" bioscope of 1901 featured a Cavioli organ powered by steam.

Spa, or spaw, is thought to come from the Old Walloon word meaning fountain. Norfolk was never in the Premiership of spa counties, but there were spas at Reffley, Oulton and Aylsham, Thetford, Shelfanger and Ditchingham; healing springs at Tottenhill, Shouldham, Great Ryburgh, Fulmodeston and North Walsham; holy wells at Walsingham, East Dereham, Bawburgh and Shadwell; and bath sea bathing at Cley, Cromer, Mundesley, Norwich, Happisburgh and Yarmouth. Sea bathing seems to have become socially acceptable in the late 1700s - at Yarmouth in the 1760s, Mundesley about 1771, Cromer about 1785, and Happisburgh in 1789. The first local official beach for nudists was established at Corton in 1979.

Credit for the first holiday camp seems to rest with John Fletcher Dodd, who died in 1952 and who was a member of the Independent Labour Party in Norwich. Its policy was to press for holidays for working people, and in 1906 Dodd took a party of 10 from London's East End to camp on land he owned at Caister. The camp consisted of three bell tents and the campers

One of Norfolk's holy wells, in the grounds of the abbey at Walsingham.

slept on straw and helped with the chores. In the early days many notable people had tenting holidays there including, so it is said, Keir Hardie, George Lansbury, and Maxim Litvinoff, the Russian-born Bolshevic and journalist, who reportedly used the name Harrison. Dodd's camp eventually evolved into Ladbroke's Caister holiday camp. Oldest established local holiday camp with a continuous history is thought to be Potters at Hopton. A surviving remnant of the original 1913 camp, a wooden hut, was ceremonially blown to bits in 1993 on the occasion of its 80th anniversary. In 1920 Herbert Potter established Britain's first permanent camp, at Hemsby, and in 1933 Mundesley holiday centre, built in the shape of a windmill motif, became the first purpose-built fully catering holiday camp in Norfolk.

The origins of the Reffley Society of King's Lynn are obscure, but the Sons of Reffley is thought to have been formed in about 1650 supposedly as a dining club for Royalists. Membership was limited to 30 as a protest against a Parliamentarian edict forbidding larger gatherings for fear of insurrection. The Le Strange family of Hunstanton and the Ffolkes family of Hillington may have had something to do with it, but in any event the Sons (or the Brethren, as they were sometimes called) maintained a tradition of free speech. The society seems to have lapsed at the Reformation and to have been re-formed in the 18th century when drinking and dining clubs were fashionable. In any event, for over 200 years it has been a wonderful slice of English eccentricity. The society seems to have originally evolved beside a spring in a wood at a farm on the Reffley estate at Wootton. By 1788, its strong social overtones intact, it possessed a stone "table," and a year later built a "temple" amid the trees. Railings and a stone circle surrounded a chalybeate spring in the centre of which was an obelisk dedicated to Bacchus and Venus. The "temple," enlarged in 1832, was a small, six-sided building guarded by two stone creatures, with a fireplace, tables, chairs, punchbowls, glasses, a rack of churchwardens' pipes, and other exotics. It was all guarded by inscribed Latin curses. Traditionally, members met annually, enjoyed a meal, smoked a pipe of special tobacco and imbibed a home-made brandy punch made from a "secret" recipe including water from the spring. The modern society's three most important officials are still President, Secretary and Brewer. Members drank toasts, laid sporting bets (one being that a certain member could drink a dozen glasses of punch in a minute), argued (a rule said no-one must ever be offended by any remark at a meeting), and meetings only ended when the President, noting the empty punchbowl, would intone the traditional closing phrase, "Gentlemen, the tide has gone out." In 1895 the Prince of Wales was a visitor, signing the book "George." And Fleet Street once descended on the wood looking for orgies. Then the Reffley calendar slowly evolved into a sort of annual sports day, members travelling from Tuesday Market Place in Lynn to play bowls, quoits and card games. In 1970 the temple was badly damaged by vandals, and the Brethren retreated into borrowed accommodation in Lynn or Hillington for the annual meet. Now the breath test reigns supreme, and the last I heard wives dutifully collected members at 10pm to drive them home. Bacchanalia was surely never like this.

In the early 1800s the ancient Maid's Head in Norwich was home base for a drinking organisation called the Everlasting Club. A popular saying was that it was easy to be admitted but more difficult to get home. The initiation ceremony apparently involved getting the prospective member drunk and then sitting him astride the wall of SS Simon and Jude church. If he fell off he was admitted as a member. If he stayed on the wall he was taken back to the Maid's Head for more refreshment.

One hundred years later, or more precisely, in 1925, Sam Vincent, a Norwich auctioneer, disappointed at the cancellation of an outing by the City Club, assembled a small group of his own and took them for the day by boat to Potter Heigham. On the way they saw a lavender field, and the name was adopted. The Lavender Club was devoted entirely to relaxation. Members, usually about 30 businessmen, according to space on board, met once a year for the sole purpose of enjoying a day out on the Broads. I was once a guest of the club and can confirm that official business was restricted to collecting subscriptions, browsing through at the minute book - the original 1925 entry, complete with group photograph, still survived - reminiscing, and listening to a brief speech by the retiring president, whose main duty was to buy a round of drinks. Official business had been known to take as little as five minutes. For the rest of the day, they enjoyed a good lunch, posed for the annual group photograph, talked, and watched the water as the hired craft plied the waterways.

The holy well of Withburga, at East Dereham, also commemorates a dark deed by the abbot and monks of Ely who, it was said, stole her body.

Norwich Number One Round Table was formed in 1927. Now the movement has thousands of members in Britain and around the world. It was created by Ermino William Louis

Marchesi, born in 1898 and the son of a Swiss immigrant, who after world war one took Langford's family restaurant in London Street, Norwich - now Moss Bros - and became a member of the Master Bakers' Association. The idea for an organisation for under-40s seems to have surfaced in 1925 when Marchesi, a Norwich Rotary Club member, stepped in for a missing speaker and suggested a club for young men. By the late 1930s Marchesi was elected a national honorary member for life, and in 1968 a memorial service for him at Westminster Roman Catholic cathedral was attended, among many others, by 10 of the original 1927 members.

Norwich Strangers Club was founded in 1928 by a group of businessmen who expressed the wish that 50 per cent of members should be "strangers," or visitors, from outside the city. The club found an outstanding home in a 16th century merchant's house in Elm Hill.

Wells Discussion Group, founded in 1931, was the last surviving group of the many formed across the country in the 1930s to listen to wireless programmes of the BBC Home Service and then discuss them. It used to be called the Wireless Discussion Group. In 1949, and tired of waiting for their wives to return from Women's Institute meetings, a group of men at Thorpe decided to form the Thorpe Men's Institute, largely devoted to talks, suppers and outings.

One of the oldest Scout groups in the country celebrated its 80th anniversary in 1988. Old Lakenham was formed in January, 1908, one year after the Scouting movement was begun by Baden Powell. Later, the group became the 1st Norwich (Capt Bowers' Own). The Women's Institute was founded at Stoney Creek, Ontario, in February, 1897. Twenty years later, in 1917, Norfolk's first branch was formed at East Runton. Friends of Kelling Hospital, formed in 1940, was the first hospital support group in the country. And one of the few all-female Morris dancing teams in the region, the Biffins, first came together in 1977.

In 1957 Harry Day founded the Young Citizen's Guild in London and begn organising holidays for London youngsters at Hemsby. The YCG remained rooted in the East London and Yarmouth areas, and members patrolled the Hemby beaches at weekends and during summer holidays, handling anything from beach cleaning, caring for lost children, and assisting the emergency services.

For some years, on or around June 21, a group of friends gathered outside a pub at Wickhampton. They were members of the Longest Day Walking Club, whose sole purpose was to walk across Halvergate marsh to the Berney Arms Inn, where they partook of refreshment prior to walking back to Wickhampton before dark. Another pub-based organisation was the East Norfolk Mountain Rescue team, which had as its motto: "We're ready, if needed." To my knowledge, they were never called.

Searching for a charity fund-raising enterprise in 1978, a Norwich lady founded the Society for the Preservation of Garden Gnomes. It was just a bit of fun, of course. But Press, radio and television all gave it national publicity and the end result was that 500 garden gnomes from all over the country had their names filed and certificated by the society.

A curious cocktail of Norfolk and Brummie accents were heard at meetings of the Norfolk Society for Birmingham and the Midlands, based at Solihull, formed over 40 years ago for exiles or relatives of Norfolk people. And in 1986 Danum comprehensive school in Doncaster formed a Bootiful Bernie Appreciation Society for Norfolk turkey chief Bernard Matthews after pupils started to adopt Norfolk accents and say things like, "bootiful."

The Greek Orthodox church in Yarmouth has an Epiphany ceremony in which the congregation processes from the church to a nearby jetty and a cross is thrown into the water. Enthusiastic members dive in - January, remember - and the finder has the honour of returning it.

The Association of Lighthouse Keepers held its inaugural meeting at Aylsham in 1988. Lighthousemen, a number of whom lived in the area at the time, considered themselves a “dying breed” because of the relentless march of automation.

To celebrate its 25th anniversary in 1987, Norfolk Amateur Radio Club set up station in the Norwich council chamber at City Hall and contacted 116 stations in 32 different countries and areas, including Germany, Alaska, Japan, Porto Rico (an island in the Indian Ocean) and Cape Horn. One member, Reg Brake, recalled tuning in to a pre-war expedition in the Congo and hearing jungle calls, and listening out for Amy Johnson when the famous flier was declared lost.

Members of the Icelandic Society of East Anglia, when they met in Norwich a few years ago to hold their annual Thorrablot, or winter feast, dined on smoked lamb and dried fish washed down with braennivin, traditional Icelandic “fire water.”

On April 27, 1792, Capt George Vancouver, of King’s Lynn, searching for Nootka Sound on the east coast of America, sailed straight passed what was subsequently called the Olympic Peninsular. He noted in his log that it was foggy at the time. In the 1960s, and on that very same spot, a new leisure and retirement community named Ocean Shores came into being. It had no traditions or history, of course, and it occurred to the then local newspaper editor, Bob Ward, that he ought to invent some. So in 1973 Undiscovery Day and the American Historical Hollering Association, known as AH-HA, came into being. The ceremony, which took place at midnight each April 27, involved residents assembling on the beach and shouting, in something like unison, “Hey, George . . .” in the hope of tempting George’s ghost ashore. Afterwards, disillusioned hollerers would drown their sorrows at the nearest waterhole. This went on for a year or two, and then the holler became famous. It was featured by a San Francisco radio station which urged its listeners to go into the streets at midnight and holler; there was a phone link with HMS Discovery moored on the Thames; former Ocean Shores’ residents living in Singapore hollered at Ocean Shores by phone across the South China Sea; and in 1982 it was written up in an American guidebook. Which is where I came in. I read it and thought, why not a holler between Ocean Shores and Vancouver’s birthplace? And so it came to pass that in April, 1983, the first ever holler took place between 65 Undiscovery Day revellers gathered in Ocean Shores’ Legend Tavern and 30 King’s Lynn Vancouver Round Tablers in the Black Horse pub at Castle Rising. At the appointed hour a phone link was established and the time-honoured ritual enacted. From Ocean Shores: “Hey, George!” And from Norfolk: “Wadda you want?” In fact, and thanks to an amplification system which enabled everyone to hear, the two groups hollered, chatted and sang to each other for half an hour or so. But the story did not end there. In April, 1985, three residents of Ocean Shores, including Bob Ward and former mayor “Bun” Lewis, flew to England just to take part in the Norfolk end of the proceedings. It was a particularly poignant holler that year. “Helluva way to come to make a phone call home,” one of them commented.

Once a week members of the Norwich Casualty Union get together to recreate realistic looking wounds on each other. The fake wounds are created to help train emergency services, hospital staffs and first-aiders. And when the police, fire and ambulance services stage training exercises union members are usually on hand to play the part of wounded casualties. In fact they pride themselves on being the only group that allows its members to "lie down and be trodden on."

Colman's of Norwich started the Mustard Club in 1926 as an advertising gimmick. But in 1991, when the club was temporarily revived, some of the original members rejoined.

The origins of British sportsmanship may go back a long way. One Roman writer recorded that although Iron Age swords were strong and unlikely to break, they were made of a soft metal. If two warriors became involved in single combat their swords would eventually begin to bend. So at a convenient moment they would step back, straighten their swords over their knees, and then begin again where they had left off.

A cricket team called Norfolk first took the field in 1797 when a match between 33 of the county and 11 of England took place at Swaffham racecourse in front of a large crowd. Despite their numerical advantage, Norfolk lost by an innings and 14 - England 144, Norfolk 50 and 80. The match apparently took the best part of a week, and Norfolk managed to record one double-figure score (14) and 35 noughts! Norfolk County Cricket Club was not formed until 1827. In 1921 the Australian touring side played a representative England XI at Old Buckenham Hall on a pitch created from turf specially brought over from Australia. Score - England 256 (Hobbs retired hurt 85), rain stopped play.

Castle Rising entertained the Italian national team in 1987. The Italians were dismissed for 47 and Castle Rising made 48-0. The Wisbech (Cambs) two-day match against the MCC dates to the mid-1920s when Maurice Tait and Jack Hobbs attended the opening of the Harecroft Road ground. One of the most famous family cricket teams was the Edrich X1, which boasted two England caps, John and Bill, and a number of county players. In 1988 the Mason family, drawn from Gooderston, Swaffham, Sporle, Hillington, Hingham and Binham, played against Castle Acre. Another Mason acted as umpire.

In 1985 Kendrick Plant Hire cricket team, of King's Lynn, challenged Lynn Chamber of Trade. The chamber accepted on condition they could nominate the pitch. They chose a Wash sandbank. The game was played in September between high tides. Two years later, members of the Lowestoft Cruising Club and the Royal Norfolk and Suffolk Yacht Club played a cricket match on Scroby Sands. A flotilla of boats went out, and the 90-minute game was won by the Yacht Club whose batsmen had the advantage of shots hit into the incoming tide.

East Winch cricket pitch is within a designated Site of Special Scientific Interest. At Narborough, the park cricket pitch has the 4ft high Devil's Dike running across the outfield.

Norwich City Football Club's antecedents seem to have been a club called Norwich FC founded in 1868. They played in Newmarket Road and their colours were "violet and black jersey and stockings, white knickerbockers, violet, black and yellow cap and tassel." This, of course, was 20 years before the Football League was formed. Norwich FC seems to have disappeared by the 1880s, and it was followed by Norfolk & Norwich Wanderers (1880s), Norwich City Swifans (1890s), and finally Norwich City (1902).

The colours by this time were "blue and white halves, blue shorts." Season 1925/26, incidentally, saw the club's first sponsored charity match, against Spurs, the fixture having been arranged by brewers Greene King. By this time the City players had a canary sewn on their shirts. Yellow and green colours seem to have been adopted, too. City used their first ever substitute on August 31, 1965, at Ashton Gate, against Bristol City. In the 70th minute Gordon Bolland, wearing an unnumbered shirt, took the field to replace the injured Terry Anderson.

The FA Cup was first held in 1871, but for Norwich the quest for glory did not begin until 1902 when the City team, formed only three weeks before, took the field at Crown Meadow, Lowestoft. The club appeared in the 1st round proper for the first time in season 1905/06, when they lost 5-0 to Tonbridge after a 1-1 draw. Norfolk's interest in the FA Cup, however, began as early as 1889 when Norwich CEYMS and Thorpe entered. The results were: Old St Marks (London) 5 Norwich CEYMS 5; replay, also in London, OSM 2 CEYMS 1 (after extra time); Thorpe 4 Old Harrovians 2; and Thorpe 2 Royal Arsenal 2 (after extra time; Royal Arsenal awarded the tie after Thorpe withdrew). In 1901 CEYMS thrashed Bury 16-0, though Bury had only eight men; and in 1906 King's Lynn were drawn at home to Aston Villa, the holders of the trophy. Lynn relinquished home advantage, the game was played in Birmingham, and Villa won 11-0.

Norwich City fans' anthem, "On the ball, City" is one of the Premiership and Football League's few true club songs. Other songs have been adopted by clubs, but this one is thought to have been composed by Albert Smith, a club director in 1905-07. And generations of the Allison family have been City groundsmen. It began with Russell, senior, who had 28 years at the Nest. One son, Roy, worked for City for 25 years, while Russell junior's links began in 1946. Russell junior's son, also Russell, carried on the tradition.

New Year's Day, 1986, was an unusually busy one in several Norfolk maternity homes and hospitals. Most patients kept mum about it, but someone finally pointed out that this particular baby bulge had arrived exactly nine months after Norwich City's Wembley victory in the Milk Cup.

Fakenham football team is known as the Ghosts. The story goes that a donkey which once lived in Fakenham Magna, Suffolk, was immortalised in verse by the poet Robert Bloomfield (1766-1825). The last four lines read: "A favourite the Ghost became/ And 'twas his fate to thrive/ And long he liv'd and spread his fame/ and kept the joke alive." For some reason, Norfolk's Fakenham adopted the nickname.

Aslacton football team endured one of the unluckiest tours of recent years. In 1985 members left by bus for a three-week visit to Russia, but the gear linkage broke down near the German border, then there was a small fire. They were stopped for speeding on their first night in Russia, ran out of diesel, and the battery went flat. Then the big end blew, the fixtures in Moscow were cancelled because of bad weather, and the team's visas ran out before a replacement bus engine arrived. Most of the team travelled back to England by rail.

Hunstanton FC and East Fulham Sports Club first competed for the Old Tin Can, a workman's beer can, in 1938. Hunstanton reserves have competed regularly for the Heath-Belding Cup, named after two world war one comrades who started the fixture.

Facade of the Hippodrome Circus at Yarmouth, one of the very few surviving indoor circus arenas in the country.

When Blickling Golf Club was disbanded in 1988 it was recalled that 57 years earlier an Aylsham member had hit a shot an estimated 1000 yards. In 1931, Walter Wade, on the 8th, apparently sliced a tee shot which bounced on the frozen lake and ran to the far end before stopping. In 1983, at Barnham Broom, a golfer hit a No 3 iron off the 17th, the ball landing in water and killing a fish. And in 1986, when Feltwell Golf Club took over the course at RAF Feltwell, the hazards included old rocket launch pads. Sutton Bridge (Lincs) nine-hole course is in the former dock basin.

There was a nice golfing moment in 1990 when the world famous Ryder Cup was taken from its cupboard at The Belfry and brought to Norfolk specially to mark the 100th birthday of Arthur England, who was still playing regularly at the Yarmouth and Caister club and who at the time was the oldest regular player in the country.

On April 30, 1876, six gentlemen dressed in grey tunics and knickerbockers, and wearing cloth helmets, set off on the Norfolk and Norwich Bicycle Club's first ever road race. They left the Grapes pub in Norwich and completed a 24-mile circuit along Unthank Road to Wymondham and then through Wicklewood, Carleton Forehoe, Colney and Earlham to Earlham Road. Winning time is unknown, but the winner was J Campling.

The late Rex Coley, of Heacham, who wrote for a cycling magazine under the name Ragged Staff, was the first journalist granted the sport's highest honour, a place in the Golden Book of Cycling. He once told me he had cycled 100,000 miles by 1930, and he remained in the saddle into his 80s. Ivan Jeckell, of Norwich, who had heart bypass surgery in 1981, clocked up 300,000 miles in 1993 after 40 years of pedalling.

I have a record of a correspondence chess match between Norfolk (Col Green and W Newton) and New York (Col Mead and J Thompson) which ended, in June, 1842, in victory in 29 moves for New York.

An extraordinary hand was reported to have been dealt at the Queen Victoria pub, at the corner of Adelaide Street and Nile Street, Norwich, in 1973. Four regulars were playing solo whist and one apparently dealt all four a complete suit of cards. The odds against this happening were said at the time to be 2,235,197,406,895,366,368,301,599,999-1.

What was believed to be the longest single chapter in Norfolk bowls history came to an end in 1964 when the George Hotel, Dereham, turned its green into a car park. Bowls was said to have been played there for 300 years.

Walking was once more competitive than it is now. A Norfolk man by the name of D Crisp, who claimed to be champion of England, in 1802 walked 40 miles a day backwards for seven days, and in 1817 covered 60 miles in 13hr 10min. In 1816 another Norfolk man, George Wilson, walked 50 miles in 11hr 45min round and round the Prussia Gardens in Lakenham. And in 1877 a Norwich man named Howes walked 22 miles 20 yards in three hours. They called themselves pedestrians in those days, incidentally. More recently, in 1994, Terry Hedger of Runcton Holme was one of a group of charity fund-raisers who walked the 31 miles from France to England through the Channel Tunnel, the first people to do so in modern times.

It was reported in 1986 that anglers were catching some individual fish so regularly that they had been given names. One of the most famous was Big Dora, a pike, caught four times in 12 months in the Upper Thurne. It appeared to have done her no harm. Between October and January, Big Dora's weight increased from 38lb to over 41lb.

The Siberian Husky Club meets during the winter months in Thetford forest, when teams ranging from two to six dogs pull special wheeled rigs at speeds up to 30mph. One of the competitions is for the Musher of the Year Cup. Swaffham Coursing Club, founded by Lord Orford in 1776, was the oldest in the country.

Hunstanton Croquet Club is over 80 years old, and various international matches have been played there. Cromer open lawn tennis championships were founded in 1908. In the 1920s and 1930s, particularly, famous players from all over the world appeared there.

Hashing is a relatively new sport in this area. Briefly, a "hare" lays out a course by leaving dabs of flour on a five-mile route across the countryside and the runners, starting later, follow the trail. There is always a pub at the end of the rainbow, I believe. Hashing is said to have begun in the 1930s when ex-patriots in Malaya organised a cross-country run with a marked out course and a pint or two when it was all over.

A four-mile swimming race in the river Ouse from St Germans to King's Lynn attracts many starters. For a number of years swimmers were accompanied in their endeavours by an inquisitive seal. And in 1985 the UEA sub-aqua club played a 10-hour marathon game of underwater draughts at Dereham swimming pool.

Dwile flonking has spread as far as New Zealand. This "ancient" pastime is actually said to have been conceived as a fund-raiser in the Waveney Valley in 1966. A team game, it revolves around a dwile (Norfolk dialect for dishcloth) which is hurled, using a driveller (stick) at fellow players. Quantities of ale also figure in the ceremony. Anyway, in 1966 Beccles hosted what was claimed to be the first ever dwile championship; and it made national headlines in 1967 when a Bungay magistrate, considering an application for a late licence for flonkers, admitted that he could not tell a dwile from a flonk.

A few years ago there was an appeal from the island of San Juan, off Vancouver Island, to the ferret-leggers of East Anglia. A trans-Atlantic ferret-legging challenge match was the hoped-for outcome. Alas, there were no local takers, which was surprising because the only equipment needed was a pair of trousers, two pieces of string, a ferret and a lot of courage. Ferret racing does emerge occasionally, however. Eye (Suffolk) has staged championship races (the ferrets run through tubular pipes) for a number of years, with the ferret Olympiad being staged in the Queen's Head car park.

Gnurdling was played at The Lifeboat pub in Thornham. It involved tossing brass discs, or coins, into a hole in a pub seat. This particular version was probably introduced during world war two by men stationed at RAF Bircham Newton, but the game itself is undoubtedly older and may have been popular at several Norfolk pubs at the turn of the century and just after.

Great Hockham's "dunking horns" are a throw-back to the old Hockham Horn Fair, which died out many years ago. Until the 1850s the horns - a helmet adorned with steer horns - were used to "dosh" strangers at the fair. They were carried in procession and hung on a wall by the village elders. Newly-weds and strangers entering the village were given free entry only if they bumped their heads against the horns. The horns were rediscovered many years ago, handed to the old Thetford Borough Council, put in store and forgotten. In 1973, however, Great Hockham got them back.

Plastic duck racing has gained in popularity over the years. In 1985 the Great Nene Duck Race was hit by disaster when most of the 1058 plastic ducks were caught by the tide and dispersed in the general direction of the Wash. Only 30 were recovered.

Congham snail racing championships have been held for over 20 years. In 1986 Solarium Sal, found at the back of a garage, beat 119 rivals to lift the trophy, competing the 13in course in the then world record time of 2min 51sec. Two years later Tracker (whose six-year-old trainer lived in Grimston) ignored a wet and soggy course, and the effects of 10 elimination heats, to set a blistering time of 2min 31sec. And in 1992 the final was won by Humpty Dumpty in 2min 23sec, only 3sec outside the record. A Surrey man once imported a box of French snails, but only one of the foreigners made the final.

Over 1200 enthusiasts built a three-and-a-half mile sand castle at Yarmouth in 1987 which snaked from Wellington Pier, past the Pleasure Beach, and ended near South Denes caravan park. It was 18,656ft long and took two-and-a-half hours to measure with a surveyor's tape.

Geoffrey Harvey of Diss was thought to be the first man to circumnavigate Norfolk by water. In 1986, he left Redgrave Fen on a 209-mile journey by canoe and dinghy. One section of the Little Ouse river was impassable, and he had to drag the canoe for half a mile. But he completed the journey in 10 days. Motorcyclist Lance Jones, of Thrandeston, near Eye, jumped 90ft from Suffolk into Norfolk in 1986. In fact he "jumped" the river Waveney at Billingford on a 250cc stunt bike with the help of a ramp.

There is a long tradition at Beccles of a sergeant-at-mace for the mayor, and indeed, the town's maces date from the 16th century. Bungay has elected a Town Reeve since at least 1725.

In 1994 a mince pie belonging to Bob Smith, a quality assurance manager, clocked up 26,175 flying miles in two months. Tucked into its travelling box, it made the acquaintance of pilots who all signed documents as to travel authenticity, and snapshots were taken of the pie relaxing in hotspots across the world. Known as Nan's Mince Pie, it is probably the only pie to have seen Germany and South Africa in one day. Apparently an Arsenal supporter, the pie was also taken on the pitch at Highbury. But it has a rival.

In 1980 an abandoned house brick on a Sardinian airfield was picked up by an airman and brought back to RAF Coltishall, whereupon Flying Officer Luigi Stanford Brick was adopted as mascot by 41 Squadron. The episode started as a joke, but FO Brick was later given an honorary rank (Service number G8131127) and flying kit. He quickly clocked up 1000 flying hours, including leading a flypast over Buckingham Palace, partnering Prince Andrew in a Sea King helicopter, and flying supersonic in Concorde. By 1991, FO Brick had topped 1250 hours, added a flight in an F-15 fighter to his air experience, and had recorded more war missions than some of the Coltishall pilots.

Newspaper headlines are often fun and occasionally apocryphal, from the wartime (Churchill Flies Back to Front, and French Push Bottles Up German Rear) to the post-war (Fuchs Off to the Arctic). My all-time favourite football headline was: Queen In Brawl at Palace. Locally, Wrentham Raps Kremlin takes a bit of beating for cheek, while the legendary Seething Bride Marries Great Snoring Man, or various versions of the same, takes the biscuit.

In 1970, when the EDP celebrated its centenary, an astonishing number of No 1 editions were turned up by proud owners. Sufficient numbers, in fact, to arouse suspicion. Then it was discovered that in 1920, on the paper's 50th anniversary, facsimile copies of the No 1 edition were given away by the hundred. Later, when a jubilee booklet was produced, hundreds more copies were distributed. The problem in 1970 was how to tell the real thing from the copy. Happily, the Wrinch Factor - devised by the author after a hurried search and examination of library files - came to the rescue. At the foot of the middle column on the front page of the No 1 edition (real and facsimile) is an advertisement by and for a certain Mr Wrinch. The bottom eight to nine lines of the advertisement hold the key. Are they blurred? If so, there is a good chance the copy is a facsimile. In fact, remarkably few genuine No 1 editions of the EDP do exist.

The late Ted Ellis wrote his nature notes for the EDP for over 40 years, one of the longest ever daily serials. A weekly column with an even longer pedigree was also written in Norfolk for many years. This was Country Notebook in the Kentish Times, based in Sidcup, written by the late Constance Hall when she lived at Sea Palling. Under the penname Elvira, she wrote the column for 53 years.

Talking of newspapers, the Wild Man pub in Norwich once held a special licence which enabled it to open at 4am for night shift print and post office workers. It is said the pianist arrived at 8am and whist drives were held before breakfast.

Anglia Television's first emblem, a silver knight, which was superseded in 1988, was over 100 years old and was originally commission by the King of the Netherlands. The King was patron of the Falcon Club which met annually to compete in horse races, falconry and sports, and in 1850 he commissioned a trophy from London silversmiths. Made to represent the Black Prince, it was won by an Englishman, who brought it home. In 1959, however, Anglia TV had it slightly remodelled and adopted it as its symbol.

Moon rock used to be a big attraction at museums. Recently, at Norwich's Castle Museum, top puller for children was a 600,000-year-old piece of fossil hyena dung - still recognisible, and looking unnervingly fresh - found in 1992 in the cliffs at West Runton during the excavation of fossil elephant bones. The elephant evidently died in shallow water and hyenas had fed on the carcase. There were teethmarks on some of the bones.

7: Bits and Pieces

In January, 1991, George Foulger received a Christmas card - 45 years late. It had been to Outer Mongolia and the United States before the Post Office finally tracked him down in Attleborough. Earliest date on the envelope was December 17, 1945, when it was sent from Norwich to Mr Foulger, then in Chester where he was stationed in the Forces. Later, he was posted to Bombay, and the card seems to have attempted to follow him. After Bombay and Outer Mongolia, it turned up in 1984 in the United States. The last postmark was Diss, in 1990. Then the postman found him. In 1988, a Norwich lady received a postcard from friends who were in Switzerland when the card was written and who may have posted it in Italy. It was delivered 36 years late. Equally puzzling was the 1976 case of the pre-paid postcard "signed" in Biro which arrived at County Hall in Norwich. It was an acknowledgement of the receipt of papers relating to a planning application to erect a temporary petrol pump outside a grocery shop-cum-post office at Smeeth Road, Marshland. The planners were puzzled because, first, the card was addressed to Thorpe Road, Norwich, which county HQ had vacated years before, and second, because the application had been made on August 15, 1939 - 37 years before. The postmark was current, and at the time the card was posted the temporary pump was still in position. In 1994, however, the mail service broke all records. A letter from Sydney, Australia, took less than two days to arrive in Bury St Edmunds (Suffolk). And in 1990, a letter from Doncaster (a suburb of Melbourne) also took two days to reach Norwich. Incidentally, in 1959 Norfolk became the first county to introduce the postcode.

Norwich policemen were baffled in 1986 when a letter arrived addressed to a Lt Fusaro. Inside was a note from a Massachussets resident complimenting Lt Fusaro on his handling of an accident report. It had been sent to the wrong Norwich. The right one was Norwich, Connecticut.

Shoppers at the Tesco supermarket in Lowestoft (Suffolk) were equally baffled a few years ago by the occasional discovery of letters originally posted during the 1930s. The first, found in a shopping basket, had been posted by a woman in America in 1930. Of the subsequent letters distributed in the store, one was sent from Ithaca, New York, in 1937, while a third had been posted in Woodbridge in 1934. Two years later the mystery deepened when more old letters, again originally sent from the States in the 1930s, were found abandoned in Belle Vue park. Another letter from Oakfield, Ohio, dated 1931, appeared to be a reply to a request for penfriends.

In 1964, when a man was lowered 110ft down the well in Norwich Castle keep, he reported a layer of coins 6in deep and 5ft across. Mind you, no-one had been down to have a look for 75 years. Nowadays, no-one has to go down to collect the harvest of coins. A platform was installed which can be hauled to the surface.

A Sprowston man regularly dropped messages in bottles into the sea while on fishing trips around the Norfolk coast, and in five years he received over 50 replies from all over Europe, including one from Stavanger and another from San Sebastian. And in 1987 a Kessingland (Suffolk) angler threw a bottle into the sea off Benacre. The bottle was subsequently thought to have ended up in the belly of a shark later sold on an East African street market, because the angler received a reply from a factory engineer in landlocked Rwanda.

In 1988, three Lowestoft schoolgirls popped a note into a lemonade bottle and asked a friend to throw it into the sea. Three months later they received a reply from a Frenchman on a tiny bird sanctuary island called Ile-aux-Basques in the St Lawrence River. He sent them maps and details about the island. The girls' teachers were puzzled, but they believed the bottle must have been thrown into the water somewhere near the island.

One message in a bottle took over 50 years to arrive. In 1939, friends Gerry Roberton and Owen Murray threw a bottle, complete with message, into the sea at Seaton Carew, near Hartlepool. It was found by Tessa Large, 16, on the beach at Scolt Head - in 1994. After some detective work Tessa traced Gerry, and Owen, a missionary in Pakistan, to tell them their message had been received.

As a schoolboy on the Dutch island of Texel, Cornelius Ellen used to ride up and down the 15 miles of beach picking up flotsam and jetsam. Later, his hobby expanded to the point where he had a museum containing a unique collection, including a "No cycling" sign from Humberside. He even ran a bottle posting service. Depending on wind and tide, he reckoned deliveries to England took about 10 days.

Tales of trawlings from the seabed abound. The skipper of Lowestoft's Ripley Queen once reported that in the vicinity of drilling platforms hard-top hats and coffee bags were top of the findings list. On a trip to the Norwegian sector of the North Sea, the Ripley Queen also found an old lamp in its nets. Dating from the early days of energy exploration the lamp was covered in barnacles and marine growth, but still in working order.

When luxury liners plied the North Sea fishermen regularly brought up cutlery and crockery. Pop pirate ships contributed masses of records to the seabed. The war added a wider range of memorabilia, including cannon balls, anchors, mines, depth charges and rolls of barbed wire. The holiday season used to keep longshore boats supplied with an endless stream of bathing slippers. In 1977 a kitchen sink was said to have been hauled up, along with a fridge, a bottle of milk, a set of false teeth, a bag of coal, and a fish with "Jim" scratched on its back.

North Sea fish have developed some odd tastes. One landed at Lowestoft was found to have swallowed a still-wrapped packet of margarine. Another had gulped half a coconut. Cod have also been known to swallow plastic cups, shells, cutlery, a beach shoe, a plastic flower, and one - caught at Bacton - a Roman coin.

One day in 1986 a West Runton fisherman went to retrieve his crab pots off the local beach when he found, floating, a pair of glasses belonging to another West Runton man. The glasses had been lost on the beach, since when two tides had flowed over them.

A difference of opinion over the origin of the expression "red herring." One reference book quotes "a red herring drawn across a fox's path destroys the scent and sets the hounds at fault." Literally, presumably. Others say the expression dates from Elizabethan pamphleteer Thomas Nashe who in 1599 published an article about the Yarmouth herring fishermen. Nashe lived for a time in Yarmouth.

The former Cock pub at Ovington, near Watton, is now a private home, and in 1988 when the owners were doing renovation work they found the pub "slate." Among the chalked names was a Mr S Adcock, who owed tuppence. Hearing the story, Paul Adcock of Watton decided to clear the family name and handed over two old pennies. The owners then began a search for a Miss Cusworth, who evidently owed 2s 8d for brandy. The building was a pub from 1860 to 1925.

In 1985, a travel worn suitcase belonging to a Norfolk man arrived back from Saudi Arabia three years after having been lost by a Dutch airline. It had been all over the world and had finally come into the possession of Air Canada. Everything in the case was complete.

Sixty-two years ago a national newspaper reported that Gimingham was the "strangest village in England." The paper claimed Gimingham had no baker, butcher, fishmonger, draper, tailor, bootmaker or policeman, and no residents named Smith, Brown, Jones or Robinson. There was no doctor, chemist or dentist. There was a railway, but no station, a public room but no public house, a church but no chapel, and although next to the sea it had no proper sea view.

A few years ago a fed-up resident of Pedham, near Blofield, erected an anti-dog sign by the roadside, reading: "This is not a canine bank, Deposits are not needed, Extend your walkies just a bit, The grass has just been seeded. Be careful not to leave your card As along our path you foot-it, Or we residents who must tread here Might tell you where to put it. So now we really make our plea, Your owners must not mock it, To get past here just shake a leg, But please, dear dog, don't cock it."

Norfolk and Norwich Hospital's famed bladder stone collection includes specimens of stones from 1453 cases operated on at the hospital between 1772 and 1909.

In 1978 an open day at Halesworth (Suffolk) sewage treatment works brought to light an odd little detail which has puzzled me ever since. During the tour a guide explained in a flush of enthusiasm that the main "head," as they apparently called it, from the Halesworth catchment area occurred, rather unusually, each day between noon and 6pm. Not first thing in the morning, mark you, or even just before bedtime. The good people of Halesworth, Holton, Blyford and Wissett seemed to be creating a flow of their own.

Vandals ultimately forced a re-think over the siting of an extraordinary clock which, for a time, was sited in Chapel Field Gardens, in Norwich. Built by horologist Martin Burgess, from Essex, it was commissioned to mark the 1975 bicentenary of Gurney's Bank. The design was based on the theories of 18th century clockmaker John Harrison, who built the chronometers used by Capt Cook to map Australia and New Zealand. It took Burgess years to decipher Harrison's 1775 writings and to work out how it could be put into practice. The finished clock incorporated a lion (the city), a castle (the bank), and brass balls (money flow), a fine combination of old ideas and modern technology.

In the mid-1980s there was a bit of a do over who was responsible for the famous but fanciful statue of Boudicca at Westminster Bridge in London. Messages between the Department of the Environment, Historic Buildings (ancient monuments section) and the GLC ascertained that the GLC had got the job. Following the demise of the GLC, however, there was another row, responsibility being disputed by Thames Water, Westminster council and the Crown. The last I heard, Westminster council had agreed to give her an occasional wash and brush up. A pity the lady, for all her faults, cannot be brought to Norfolk.

A 1986 excavation of three trial holes in the keep of Norwich Castle uncovered the fact that on the north side the keep had been subject to an early construction failure which had necessitated a certain amount of rebuilding. Even this work was not entirely successful, because it was also found that in the 18th century a large repair stitch had to be inserted. I hope the stones stand firm. Among the many treasures kept there is a collection of some 2000 18th and 19th century teapots which, with the museum's own 600 teapots, makes it the largest collection of British ceramic teapots in the world.

For several decades one of the most famous "faces" in Norfolk archaeology was a chalk figurine emanating from Pit 15 at Grimes Graves flint mines. In 1960 the late R Rainbird Clarke wrote that "a pedestal of chalk blocks was surmounted by the roughly carved figurine of a pregnant female with, close by, a number of chalk balls and a carved phallus. The only reasonable interpretation . . . is that it represents the shrine of an Earth Goddess." The figure of the rotund lady was duly given an important position at the British Museum. However, the 1984 Department of the Environment's Grimes Graves booklet commented somewhat carefully: "The excavators said they had found a small crudely carved chalk figure of a woman." A more recent guidebook carried a small photograph of the lady accompanied by a cautious caption: "The chalk 'goddess.'" The quotation marks were ominous. Meanwhile, Norfolk's newest "famous face" is that of Spong Man, a human figure wearing a flat cap sitting in a chair, elbows on knees and hands against each cheek, unearthed during a dig at the Anglo Saxon cemetery site at Spong Hill. So far, Spong Man is unique.

The elaborate font at Knapton church, complete with Greek palindrome around the bottom of the canopy.

A Hoover-like mud-gulping machine was used to aid restoration of areas like Cockshoot Broad. Belaugh Broad, which once extended for 15 acres, was down to about five acres in 1987. Here, the mud-gulper sucked out 4ft of mud at a rate of 2000 gallons a minute - enough to fill Norwich City's Carrow Road football stadium to a depth of 10ft. Some years before, the same machine had pumped out the canal at Versailles, near Paris, and lakes at Windsor Castle.

When a Shotesham man's home was plunged into darkness during a storm in 1987, all he had to do was go to his garage to select which back-up generator he wanted to use. He had collected them for years. In the end he rigged up an 1897 model generator in the garden. It started first time, but he had to stand by with an umbrella in case in rained, because the generator was not covered.

Mechanical engineer Peter Pallandine of Northwold spent many years designing, building and developing a steam car. His target was to beat the world speed record for a steam car, of about 127mph, set by a Stanley Steamer over 80 years ago.

A few years ago a Barnham farmer went to answer nature's call and had just sat down when he felt an unusual and unwelcome sensation below. Looking down, he saw water squirting out of a metal pipe sticking up from the pan. Rapid retreat followed by an investigation revealed the "culprit" was a drains' clearance firm trying to shift a blockage. The rod had gone right round several bends and into the toilet where the farmer was sitting.

Talking of being spotted, Norfolk has had its share of "lights in the sky" stories. Unidentified flying object reports were at their highest in the 1950s and 1960s. The next dècade produced some strange sounds at Caister and lights at Cromer, and lights in the sky were reported at intervals throughout the 1970s-80s. In 1987, the chairman of the national Aetherius Society pleaded with Norfolk sky-watchers to "go public" about UFOs in an attempt to prove the sceptics wrong. He claimed recent sightings had included a bright object over Earlham which divided into three and disappeared, and a cigar-shaped red glow spotted in daylight from Blakeney Point. In more recent years, corn circles have also crept into the equation.

Apparently there is a distinctive piece of regional methodology in the small and occasional art of putting ships in bottles. An exponent who lived at Neatishead once told me that Norfolk's "du different" approach was upheld by using a staple to swivel the mast. Bottlers elsewhere generally used pins, apparently.

Norwich Puppet Theatre, based at a converted church, has a heightened problem every time it wants to put up its Christmas lights or change a bulb in the roof. Even the longest ladders will not reach. So they call in Norwich Climbing Club, whose members rig ropes and tackle and use the opportunity for a spot of useful practice.

Lions Club members on a car treasure hunt in Sheringham Woods on a Sunday in 1988 came across an unscheduled clue. A professional photographer and his scantily-clad model had found a secluded spot for a back-to-nature photo session. Alas, when the first of the treasure seeking cars arrived there had to be a hurried covering-up of the model, a sequence repeated at regular intervals when the other 17 cars turned up, one by one.

Engineer David King, of Suffield, has produced some marvellous machines over the years, including a steam-driven car. One of the most intriguing was a steam driven-gramophone, named the Fogrophone. A prototype made a debut appearance at Bodham, but it was not until a steam rally at Taverham in 1976 that the Fogrophone first appeared in public in all its steam/musical glory.

In 1990, some 45 pythons - a British record - were brought together at Norwich's Hewett School as part of Thorpe Aquarist Society's show. For the record, there were 16 Indian pythons, 25 Royals and four reticulated. The biggest was Tiny, which measured 17ft and weighed 10st.

A palindrome reads the same backwards as it does forwards - hence the first words to Eve: "Madam, I'm Adam." There is a more complicated one on the font at Knapton church. Written in Greek, it is said to have been composed by the Emperor Leo (880-911). In English, it roughly translates as: "Wash my sins and not my face only." Still on the subject of churches, Burnham Deepdale has a remarkable Norman "seasonal" font, carved on three sides with figures and activities representing the changing year; while on the choir stalls at Salthouse, among the scratchings and pieces of graffito, are lots of crude yet remarkable representations of 17th century vessels.

Supermarket trolleys are an unusual form of litter, but a few years ago more than 40 were pulled out of the water from King's Lynn's Millfleet and Purfleet. And in another clean-up, dozens were also dragged out from the water at Thetford's shopping centre. Talking of litter, visitors to the Royal Norfolk Show regularly drop 25 tons of rubbish in two days over the showground. As for Norfolk people in general, someone once calculated they create enough refuse every six weeks to fill the whole of County Hall.

A huge bed evidently built for state visits to Raynham Hall, near Fakenham, in 1713, was rediscovered packed in boxes in 1990 and subsequently bought by Hampton Court palace. The bed measured 19ft 6in.

Gateley, in South West Norfolk constituency, was one of the county's smallest polling locations. With no public building in the village the polling station is sometimes a council house or, as in 1987, a farmhouse. In 1988. Gateley had 30 names on its electoral roll. Several villages have a smaller number of voters, but they do not necessarily have a polling station of their own. Tottington and Stanford, in the Battle Area, have no voters at all. Villages which do not possess a public building have to look elsewhere for a polling station. At Attlebridge, part of the church was used.

Nationally, many MPs receive about 10,000 letters a year. A few years ago a Norwich MP revealed he received up to 30 letters a day, within which animals easily topped the subject list - animal charities, animal welfare, and dogs fouling footpaths. This particular interest was underlined when an environmental poll run in Norwich by the UEA branded dog owners and vandals as city enemies Nos 1 and 2. But dog dirt raised more hackles than anything else.

There are at least three ships depicted by these crude scratchings in the woodwork at Salthouse church.

In 1987 voters at Suffield had an opportunity to elect a new parish council for the first time in more than 30 years. Earlier, Suffield councillors had decided not to stand for re-election. Said one: "We're almost a prehistoric village, and we more or less elect ourselves. I've never known an election here. We're a remote hamlet that's hardly on the map, and having an

Another example of the remarkable Medieval shipping graffito to be found at Salthouse church.

election is really quite sensational." But in 1987 North Norfolk District Council insisted. When nominations closed, there were 11 candidates for the seven seats.

The University of East Anglia's Students' Union vote for a new secretary got itself into a bit of a tangle in 1988. Problems first surfaced in 1986 when the Rag Week Society candidate, a goldfish, finished fourth. Then in 1987, Trevor, a Christmas tree, came third. In 1988, however, Kenneth the gerbil topped the poll with a 100-vote majority. The University refused to let the newly elected student leader take control of the union's £250,000 budget and a chain of shops, or negotiate changes in student residences and social facilities. Kenneth, owned by a student, finally resigned and a second ballot took place.

8: End Pieces

Long distance love helped solve a crime a year or two ago. A Norwich man was talking on the telephone to his girlfriend in New Zealand when she told him that burglars were trying to smash their way through her front door. He immediately hung up and made another call, ultimately convincing the New Zealand police it was not a hoax and that there really was a burglary in progress. They were on the scene within minutes and one of the culprits was arrested. In a subsequent hearing in New Zealand, the bemused court heard how the emergency call had been made from England.

A vintage motorcycle enthusiast who lived near Dereham parked a Brough Superior in London in 1967 only to find later that it had been stolen. In 1987, a British dealer decided to buy a bike advertised for sale by "an ex-motorcycle enthusiast" who lived just outside New York. The seller claimed he had brought it in Brooklyn in 1970. The dealer checked with the Brough Superior Owners' Club and discovered it was the stolen 1930s 680cc V-twin. Later, a contact in America bought back the bike.

Wymondham Petty Sessions book of 1886 contained references to a prisoner "drunk whilst in charge of horse and cart," and to fare dodging on the local railway.

The first Crimestoppers' campaign was launched in 1983 by Yarmouth police and the Yarmouth Mercury. By the end of 1988 it had accounted for 300 crimes, resulting in 78 people being arrested and charged, and had paid out £3500 in reward money.

In 1988 peace campaigner Angie Zelter, of East Runton, sought an arrest warrant against the Prime Minister for allegedly threatening to kill thousands of Russians. Mrs Zelter gave evidence on oath to a magistrate at Cromer, presenting statements from academics, lawyers, doctors and a journalist. Her application failed.

A repentent shoplifter paid for some stolen sweets 15 years after the event. In 1988 a former Lowestoft shopkeeper received an envelope containing a £5 note and an unsigned letter confessing to the theft and asking for forgiveness. That same year a couple appeared hand-in-hand before North Walsham magistrates' court having super-glued themselves together. They had to sit on either side of the dock with their hands still together, and it was three hours before they were separated.

For many years, public hangings in Norwich were carried out in the market place. Later, executions at the old Castle Hill prison invariably drew huge crowds. In the 19th century railway excursions from outlying areas brought trippers in to witness the spectacle. A few minutes before noon the death knell was tolled at St Peter Mancroft. A bag was then placed over the head of the victim who died on a gallows erected between the two stone lodges at the entrance to the castle bridge. Norwich's last public execution, in 1849, was that of James Rush, the Stanfield Hall murderer, and the last execution at the Castle was that of Hubbard Langley in 1867. The underground passage built in 1820 to link the castle jail with the then new Shirehall courts still exists, and links the present museum to the Royal Norfolk Regimental Museum. Last man to walk through the passage and climb the spiral staircase back to the castle with the death sentence ringing in his ears was George Harmer in 1886.

Norwich Prison on Mousehold Heath was also equipped for executions, and indeed, carried them out until the 1950s. It originally had a condemned cell and an execution room with a double beam. The room was later converted into an office.

King's Lynn had a particularly gruesome method of dealing with criminals. It boiled them to death. In 1531 an Act legalised the use of the caldron, and that year a Lynn maid was duly sentenced. While being dipped in and out of the boiling liquid, it is said her chest burst open and her heart was propelled against the wall of a house on the far side of Tuesday Market Place. The place where the heart is said to have landed is marked by a small diamond-shaped brickwork insignia containing a heart design which is still to be seen above the middle upstairs window of a house overlooking the market.

In 1988, archaeological excavations in West Norfolk uncovered 80 skeletons in what was thought to have been an 8th to 10th century Saxon cemetery. In the ring ditch which surrounded it dozens more skeletons were found, some three deep, some lying on their stomachs or with their legs doubled up. They may have been outcasts or criminals who had been hanged or decapitated. Under Danelaw, blood money could be paid, but the Saxons inflicted capital punishment for crimes against the person, and believed in an eye for an eye. The area may have been a judicial centre. One of the largest Saxon cemeteries known in Norfolk is the early Saxon graveyard at Spong Hill, near North Elmham. Excavated between 1972-81, it produced over 2000 cremations.

A few years ago a former Norwich man was murdered in Riyadh, Saudi Arabia, and a Saudi man was later arrested. The Saudi man's family accepted that he was responsible. Thus, under Saudi law, the Norwich man's parents were given a choice of demanding the death penalty or accepting a payment in kind. It is believed they chose the latter.

Still on the subject of executions, there is a gibbet in the Norwich Castle Museum dungeon which still has bits of skull sticking to it. Incidentally, the museum also has the severed hand of Norfolk squire Sir John Hayden, who lost it in a duel near Norwich in 1600. And it was rumoured the body of a bear was buried under a flowerbed in the Castle gardens a few years ago, purely in the interests of research. The bear had died at an animal park and the skeleton will be studied in years to come.

Wymondham's Bridewell has its place in history. The first building, which may have incorporated dungeon-like cells, was re-built in 1785. The new building contained 21 individual cells, a concept so new it caused great excitment among the judiciary, and magistrates and gentlemen from afar came to visit. Wymondham jail is also credited with being the inspiration behind the first penetentiary in the United States. Some 40 years after it was built, however, Wymondham's "new" Bridewell was empty and up for sale - for the first time.

In June, 1985, the then Home Secretary opened the new Wayland Prison at Griston, built at a cost of £18.7 million. Two months later the first two prisoners escaped, using metal hooks and webbing to scale the perimeter fence. Norwich's so-called New Prison on Mousehold Heath opened in August, 1887, but it was not until the following February that two prisoners escaped from a working party in the grounds.

When four skeletons were unearthed by building contractors near Diss, the bones and some coins also unearthed were confirmed as dating from the Roman period. Some time later the bones were re-interred in St Andrew's churchyard, Scole, but not before the rector had thumbed through his books to find out how to deal with a burial 1800 years late. The four citizens of Roman Britain were eventually given a Christian burial and a plot near the church front door.

One of the biggest society funerals ever seen in Norfolk was that of Coke of Holkham in 1842. When the hearse drew up at the door of the church "the line of carriages alone reached Litcham, two-and-a-half miles away." And there were enormous crowds at the 19th century funeral of Jeremiah Colman, known as a benevolent employer. The city came to a standstill and 1200 employees followed the coffin.

In the early 1980s helicopter pilots flying out of Yarmouth and Bacton were puzzled by an unusual pattern visible in Long Gore Marsh between Hickling and Sea Palling. It appeared to have been cut in the waterlogged marsh and seemed to resemble a king-sized crown with letters beneath. In fact the design was a double-headed eagle holding a Greek cross with the letter M. More specifically, it represented an ancient emblem of Greece which was also the symbol of the Vlastos family from the Aegean island of Chios. It was cut in the early 1960s and marks the place where the ashes of Marietta Pallis were interred after her death in 1963. Later, the ashes of her companion were also interred there. Miss Pallis, a gifted botanist and artist, lived at Long Gores, Hickling, for many years.

The Rosary cemetery in Thorpe Hamlet, Norwich, full of grave Victorian melodrama, was a pioneer "private" cemetery for those outside the Established Church.

Burial at sea is unusual nowadays, but not unknown. Norfolk sea burials are made at a point some 20 miles off Yarmouth, in a specially designated area. Strict rules are applied by, of all people, the Ministry of Agriculture. In 1987 the

The Scole memorial to some local citizens of Roman Britain.

ashes of Herb Miller, brother of bandleader Glenn Miller, were scattered into the North Sea off Lowestoft. Herb took the band all over the world to keep Miller music alive, and his outfit was a regular attraction at Pontin's Holiday Camp at Pakefield.

The Rosary cemetery at Thorpe Hamlet, Norwich, full of Victorian melodrama.

At Martham church was a slab - hidden from view by the organ, alas - to Christopher Burraway who died in 1730, aged 59, and his wife Alice, died 1729 aged 76, "who by her life was my sister, my mistress, my mother and my wife." The story goes that farmer's daughter Alice had a son who was sent away to a foundling hospital. The son grew up and came back to Martham where the lady of the farm - by now Alice - hired him as a labourer. He became farm steward, duly married his mistress, and became church warden. One day Alice realised he was her son, and died of shock. Christopher died a few months later. A more simplistic view, incidentally, is that he married his stepfather's widow.

The children born to Sarah and Daniel Hill between 1808 and 1835 were buried side by side at Wrentham (Suffolk) - all 11 of them. Most of the children did not see their first birthday, but the last gravestone was that of an 11-year-old girl. At Tilney All Saints there is a grave reputed to be that of Tom Hickathrift, a fabled strong man who is said to have lived in the marshland at the time of the Normans. It is claimed he performed many feats of strength, though only the oral legend and an unmarked stone slab remain.

The South Creake bier, built in 1688, was "rediscovered" in the church belfry a few years ago and promptly described by Victoria and Albert Museum experts as "one of the finest three in the country."

War cemeteries abound all over the world, and there are War Graves Commission cemeteries from two world wars - impeccably maintained - throughout Europe, North Africa and the Far East. Simularly, a few German graves are to be found at several locations in Norfolk, mostly near air bases.

A pyramid-shaped mausoleum in the grounds of Blickling Hall contains the remains of John Hobart, 2nd Earl of Buckinghamshire, who lived at the Hall. He was the grandson of Henry Hobart, killed in a duel in 1698. Sir John died in 1793. A stone marking the site of the 1698 duel can be found about a mile east of Cawston beside the B1149. Attleborough is said to have had a pyramid-shaped gravestone, too. It was dedicated to solicitor Melanothon William Henry Lombe Brooke, who died in 1929 and who left precise measurements for the stone in his will. At Grimston, the last resting place of a blacksmith was marked by an anvil-shaped stone.

Whissonsett has a village memorial to the Seagrim brothers, one of whom was awarded the George Cross, the DSO and the MBE, and the other the Victoria Cross. Lt Col Derek Seagrim served in North Africa, and Major Hugh Seagrim in Burma, where he is remembered today. A folk hero to the Karen hill tribesmen, and remembered by them as "Daddy Longlegs," Hugh Seagrim fought with them against the Japanese. He voluntarily surrendered in an effort to stop Japanese reprisals and was subsequently executed in Rangoon.

Elveden's (Suffolk) world war one memorial, a substantial landmark on the A11, was unveiled in 1921 by Field Marshal Sir Henry Wilson. It stands at the meeting point of the parishes of Elveden, Eriswell and Icklingham and is 127ft high.

Costessey's Roundwell monument, restored in the 1980s, was built in 1820 by French prisoners of the Napoleonic war. It is thought to be unique in design, being built on top of a spring and comprising an obelisk and urn. Attleborough has a fine Crimean War memorial, complete with lampholders and mileages to nearby towns.

Epitaphs abound. Here are a couple. St John Maddermarket (recorded): "Here snug in her grave my wife doth lie. Now she's at rest and so am I." Martham: "Though shot and shell flew fast on Balaclava's Plain, Unscathed he passed to fall at last, Run over by a train."

Aeronautical memorials abound, too. A cairn in a field at Bacton; a plaque on a channel marker in Blakeney harbour; a wooden cross in Buxton Great Wood; Spitfire Marsh at Claxton; a plaque in farm buildings at East Harling; a cross on the edge of a cornfield at Gawdy Hall, near Harleston; a Liberator bomber on the Rackheath village sign; and so on.

In the 1970s a cross at Swaffham dedicated to a lady who died in 1837, and situated between the Sexton's House and the church, gained a certain notoriety when it was discovered that it had moved. In the seven years since gradual movement was first noted and regularly measured, it turned fully 90 degrees. The tale came to an end in 1981, however, when the turning cross was smashed by vandals.

New milestones are unusual these days. One of the last to be erected was at Thurton, in 1985. Made locally of cast iron, it was erected as a private memorial to Arnall and Elizabeth Capps, who died in 1960.

American world war two airman Harry Stien, from New Jersey, who flew a Liberator named Blood and Guts, returned to his former base at Old Buckenham in 1987 to find himself listed as dead on a plaque in the Memorial Room. During the war his plane was shot down in the North Sea. Six of the crew died but others, including Mr Stien, were picked up by a minesweeper. "At least they spelled my name right," he quipped.

The former air base at North Creake once had a particularly poignant memorial. In 1944, Flt Engineer Ted Allen of 199 Squadron painted a mural featuring a Stirling bomber which was later lost in an operation over the North Sea. Afterwards, someone added, "Chop. 16-4-44. RIP," to the mural. It survived until 1983 when members of the Fenland Aircraft Preservation Society cut out the section of wall and delivered it to the RAF Bomber Command museum at Hendon.

Mysterious vibrations crop up every now and again. In 1986 there were complaints from the Cantley area of rumblings and shakings. And 1988 brought at least two separate complaints of booms, bangs or wobblings, generally thought to have been connected with aircraft. One of the most famous was the Worlingham "hum," first reported in 1981. Variously described as "a humming" or a "faint, faraway foghorn," the bulk of local reports seemed to emanate from an area around three streets.

Attleborough's fine Crimean War memorial, complete with lamp brackets and mileages to nearby towns.

During world war one Canon Reginald Bignold, of Carlton Colville (Suffolk), regularly noted in his diary that the sound of guns could be heard from across the Channel and that artillery barrages in France and Flanders were plainly discernible. In 1916 a massive explosion at Faversham (Kent) powder factory, in which 70 people died, was clearly felt in Norfolk where doors and windows rattled.

Lots of ghostly happenings in the area, but two will suffice. In 1987 a physic researcher claimed to have communicated with the spirit of an Italian woman who is said to haunt the auditorium of the Norwich Theatre Royal. Breakthrough to "the other side" came when the medium used automatic writing by holding a pen to paper and allowing it to write. The spirit evidently said her name was Jane Felina and that she used to live on the site of the theatre. Theatre staff had already reported seeing doors opening and closing, and cleaners had mentioned alarming experiences when doors slammed for no apparent reason. A year earlier, ghostbusters investigated three spectral squash-playing airmen at Bircham Newton. The site of the old airfield is now the Construction Industry Training Board, but the courts were built during world war one. One court is said to be colder than its neighbour, and the hauntings are reported to have begun during the last war when three squash-mad airmen crashed in their bomber near Bircham Newton church. In more recent years there has evidently been a sighting of an airman in full flying gear, and sound recordings - taken at night - of footsteps, noises on court, and a bomber pilot talking to the control tower with the drone of engines in the background.

One ghost gave up. In 1937 Dunston was in a frenzy of excitment after a driver reported seeing a white spectre in his headlights on a late night drive. The sighting made newspaper headlines and was well remembered. In 1986, however, when Charlie Blackburn and his wife Ellen celebrated their diamond wedding, Charlie confessed: "The ghost was me, poaching, wearing a white sheet." Only his family and poaching partner knew the truth, and no one said a word. Not for nearly 50 years, anyway.

In 1985 a popular reproduction picture of a crying urchin was linked to a spate of fires across the country. The picture was said to be cursed. One national newspaper organised a bonfire of 800 copies of the painting. When a Norwich man decided to collect copies of the "Crying Boy" picture he received 30 replies to his advertisement fom the Norwich area. Earlier, there had been reports of fires in Merseyside and elsewhere in which similar portraits had been present, but left untouched. One fire which fuelled local speculation was at a pizza restaurant in Yarmouth. The "Crying Boy" was hanging only feet away from where the blaze began, but it was untouched by smoke or flames. Firemen blamed the outbreak on an electrical fault.

It is sometimes said that radio transmissions can occasionally be picked up by such bizarre receivers as gold teeth and teeth fillings. Once, when living in Thorpe Hamlet, in a lofty position above Norwich, I regularly picked up a French radio station on loudspeakers connected to a record player. Even more bizarre, though unhappily unconfirmed, was a rumour that a resident in a Housing Association flat in the city regularly had music coming from his toilet. He declined to be interviewed on the subject.

Natural nuisances are fairly familiar. "Shrimps" in tap water at Yarmouth; Spanish moon moths at Barnham in 1986; swarms of thunder flies which set off fire alarms; greenfly invasions at Cromer, Holt, Sheringham and Yarmouth in 1986; and clouds of relatives of the cockchafer, known locally as buzz-bombs or blind bees, at Lowestoft also in 1986. Three years later there were reports of strange odours invading the coast between London and Colchester, and in due course the "farmyard-type smell" reached Lowestoft. Most noticeable during a strong easterly wind, the Euro-pong was thought to be the result of intensive farming methods in Holland, Belgium or France.

On May 2, 1986, a radiation cloud from the Russian nuclear power station disaster at Chernobyl passed over East Anglia at a height of 2000ft. A great deal of pollution of all types swirls over Europe. In 1985 a grey "snow" which settled on Norwich was thought to have been caused by pollution from Soviet power stations.

9: And Finally, the Future

The fastest population growth in England looks likely to continue in East Anglia. Based on 1985 projections by the Office of Population, Censuses and Surveys, this means a growth in regional (East Anglian) populations from 1.9 million to 2.26 million by the year 2001. Using similar calculations, Norfolk's population seems likely to grow to about 900,000 by the year 2011. Even the Structure Plan allows for a Norfolk population of 834,000 by 2006. It is similar to the addition of a town the size of King's Lynn, or 10 Swaffhams. And a 1986 survey predicted that the population of Norwich's travel-to-work catchment area would top 350,000 by about 2006. By then, King's Lynn would have grown to 12,000 and Yarmouth to 11,000.

There are also shifts in the age structure of Norfolk's population. One set of Government figures suggested that in the 15-29 young, free and single group, the number of men was exceeding the number of women. At the other end of the scale, however, there were more Joans than Darbys, though the situation may have evened out by 2001.

The influx has done funny things to roads already creaking under the strain of rising vehicle ownership. And there is worse to come. Long distance projections suggest an annual rise of 13 per cent in the number of vehicle registrations.

In 1986 Professor Tim O'Riordan of the University of East Anglia proposed taking six million acres of agricultural land out of cereal production. He said a dramatic shift in land use must take place before over-production forced further decline among the rural communities. He suggested turning some lowland areas over to productive woodland.

The present Norfolk population already produces, in six weeks, enough household rubbish to fill the inside of County Hall; but even the most modest forecasts suggest the tonnage will be much greater by the end of the century. And it is getting harder to find holes or spaces big enough in which to bury it or spread it. Talking of holes, fishermen protested a year or two ago that if sand and gravel continued to be dredged off Yarmouth then in 20 years the operations would have lowered the seabed by two inches.

Energy will continue to be a problem. Denver and Weybourne are traditionally mentioned as possible sites for new nuclear power stations, but there would be a lot of opposition. At the time of writing, however, wind power is the thing. "Wind farm" sites have sprung up and more are in the planning pipeline. Some say they are beautiful, others that they are ugly. But the real downside is that a great many are needed, they can be noisy and reflect sunlight, passers-by tend to stop their cars to gawp at them, and the "farms" have been known to interfere with television reception.

One novel attempt to find alternative energy resources concerns poultry power. The world's first commercial electricity plant generating power from chicken droppings opened in 1992 at Eye (Suffolk). At the time of writing there are plans for a second, larger plant near Thetford.

Food may become less of a problem. In 1990 it was announced that scientists at the Institute of Plant Science Research at the John Innes Institute at Colney were working on ways of taking the cabbage and sprout taste out of cabbages and sprouts. The idea was that if they could make them sweeter they would appeal to many more people, particularly children.

On a festive note, Norfolk businessman Roger Haywood has booked the Royal Albert Hall for New Year's Night, 1999, to see in the year AD2000. Among other surprises, he is evidently planning to invite everyone from his home village, Happisburgh - about 800 people - to the celebrations. Should be quite a party.

In one sense the party might more properly be a wake as it seems that not much of Norfolk will be around in the centuries to come. Climatic researchers at the UEA were asked some time ago to carry out the longest range forecast of all time by predicting what the weather patterns would be for the next million years. This was for Nirex, the Government body for nuclear waste sites, which wanted to know if its nuclear waste depositories were going to be covered by new Ice Age glaciers. Even short-term forecasting is difficult as weather patterns change so quickly. For example, UEA researchers reckon that the last but one Ice Age, which existed for more than 14,000 years, was transformed into a warm period inside 300 years, and that the plunge back into cold took only another 500 years. As for today's temperate climate, it took a mere 300 years to evolve.

Overall, global temperatures and ocean levels are rising. A 1989 forecast was that global temperatures would rise by 0.5degC by the year 2000 with an associated rise in sea levels of between 30 and 60cm by AD2030. At the same time, and because of a geological see-saw effect, southern England has been sinking for centuries, perhaps by as much as a foot every 100 years. In addition, Anglian Water once calculated that 70 per cent of the region's coastline was receding and that 80 per cent of the shoreline was getting steeper. A gradually sloping beach disperses wave power while a steep beach can mean undermined walls and defences.

Another scenario is that temperatures will start to cool again in about 300 years' time, when fossil fuels have run out; that in 3000 years' time Norfolk, along with parts of Lincolnshire, Cornwall, South Wales and bits of Shropshire and Cheshire will have vanished altogether under the waves; and that in 7000 years the north will have joined Norway and there will be another full-blown Ice Age.

The face of the future? A windfarm glowers over West Somerton churchyard.

Even if medium-term forecasts are generally correct, there will be an increasing flood threat to the coastline we have come to believe is traditional. Fenland would be under serious threat, as would stretches of shoreline from King's Lynn to Sheringham. Eroding cliffs aside, also at risk would be the coast from Happisburgh round to Beccles and as far inland as Norwich. Some of the risk would be to the low-lying parts of Yarmouth and Broadland, which would end up as a giant salt water lake inhabited by brackish water and fish. Suggestions put forward so far include planning restrictions in areas likely to be affected, more anti-erosion and storm surge defensive work, a tidal barrier, and the sacrificing of a huge section of the lower river valley to create a new system of washes, or spillways, perhaps on Haddiscoe Island, to absorb some of the flood.

A young visitor examines the flood gauge on Blakeney quay.

All this may help to explain the old jingle: "He who would old England win, Must at Weybourne Hoop begin."

It could refer to a determined invader, of course. Increasingly, though, it looks as though the real winner will be the sea.

But there is some slight hope for us and for Norfolk. In a prize-winning essay in 1993, Richard Wade-Martins, of North Elmham, in considering three possible endings of the world (meteorite strike, lack of carbon dioxide, human ignorance) concluded that we have at least 100 million years to go.

Enjoy it while you can.